In the Net

Misha Levkov

methuen | drama

LONDON • NEW YORK • OXFORD • NEW DELHI • SYDNEY

METHUEN DRAMA
Bloomsbury Publishing Plc
50 Bedford Square, London, WC1B 3DP, UK
1385 Broadway, New York, NY 10018, USA
29 Earlsfort Terrace, Dublin 2, Ireland

BLOOMSBURY, METHUEN DRAMA and the Methuen
Drama logo are trademarks of Bloomsbury Publishing Plc

First published in Great Britain 2023

A catalogue record for this book is available from the British Library.

A catalog record for this book is available from the Library of Congress.

ISBN: PB: 978-1-3503-8659-4
ePDF: 978-1-3503-8660-0
eBook: 978-1-3503-8661-7

Series: Modern Plays

Typeset by Mark Heslington Ltd, Scarborough, North Yorkshire

To find out more about our authors and books visit
www.bloomsbury.com and sign up for our newsletters.

WoLab presents . . .

In the Net

By Misha Levkov

Cast

Hala **Suzanne Ahmet**
Immigration Officer / Councillor / Estate Agent **Tony Bell**
Laura **Carlie Diamond**
Anna **Anya Murphy**
Harry **Hywel Simons**

Writer **Misha Levkov**
Director **Vicky Moran**
Set and Costume Designer **Ingrid Hu**
Lighting Designer **Jonathan Chan**
Sound Designer **Matt Eaton**
Video Designer **Daniel Denton**
Movement Director **Nadia Sohawon**
Dramaturg **Frey Kwa Hawking**
Technical Stage Manager **Max Juan-Balch**
Casting Assistant **Aoife Smyth**
Graphic Design **Ciaran Walsh for CIWA Design**

For WoLab

Creative Director **Alistair Wilkinson**
Associate Director **Kaleya Baxe**
Marketing Consultant **Holly Adomah**

With thanks to: Anne Bogart, Gemma Barnett, A.A. Brenner, Shireen Farkhoy, Simran Hunjun, Jermyn Street Theatre, Jerwood Space, Hannah Kumari, Tom Littler, India Martin, Adrianne McKenzie, Sarah Meadows, Sue Odell, Punchdrunk, RTYDS, Colm Summers, Rakhee Thakrar, Audrey Thayer, Audrey Sheffield, Lyndsey Turner, the WoLab extended family, and John Vernon.

This production was first performed at the Jermyn Street Theatre, 12 January 2023.

WoLab's other plays published by Methuen include: *For a Palestinian* by Bilal Hasna and Aaron Kilercioglu; and *Rainer* by Max Wilkinson. Other WoLab plays include: *ENG-ER-LAND* by Hannah Kumari and *Man-Cub* by Alistair Wilkinson.

Suzanne Ahmet – Hala

Suzanne is an actor working across stage, screen and voice.

Theatre credits include: Mary Baldwin, *Marvellous*, @sohoplace, transferred from The New Vic Theatre; Susan, *The Haunting of Susan A* by Mark Ravenhill, The Kings Head Theatre; Elizabeth Bennet, *Pride and Prejudice*; Mistress Page, *The Merry Wives of Windsor* and Kaa, *The Jungle Book* for Storyhouse @ GPOAT 2021; *The Ballad of Maria Marten*, Eastern Angles and Matthew Linley Creative Projects; *Homing Birds*, Kali Theatre; *Saint George and the Dragon* and *Peter Pan* for The National Theatre; *Hard Times*, Northern Broadsides; *The Hoard Festival* and *Around The World in 80 Days*, The New Vic; *The Winter's Tale*, Sheffield Crucible; *I Capture The Castle*, Watford Palace and Bolton Octagon and *Much Ado About Nothing* and *Dangerous Corner*, The Theatre Royal, Bury St Edmunds.

Screen credits include: Netflix/BBC Drama, *Inside Man*; Teva Pharmaceuticals (https://www.youtube.com/watch?v=iApPT1YWomo); *Adult Material* and *Gittins*, C4; *Doctors*, *EastEnders* and *Jonathan Creek*, BBC.

She has worked as a development artist for The New Vic (*Marvellous*); Shakespeare's Globe (*Read Not Dead* and Globe Research in Action); and The RSC (*The Boy in the Dress*). She also plays Blanca, *Into the Melting Pot* for The Telling, which is a feature film and live touring production. https://www.thetelling.co.uk/films

Tony Bell – Immigration Officer / Councillor / Estate Agent

Tony trained at the Webber Douglas Academy of Dramatic Art.

Stage credits include: *Wonderland* (Nottingham Playhouse); *Karagula* (Soho Theatre); *The Damned United* (West Yorkshire Playhouse); *Shakespeare in Love* (Noel Coward Theatre); *The Tempest* (Oxford Playhouse); *The Glee Club* (Cast Theatre) and *39 Steps* (Fiery Angel Productions); *The Winter's Tale* and *Richard III* (Propeller); *The English Game* (Headlong); *Treasure Island* (Royal Haymarket); *A Man For All Seasons* (Haymarket); *Ghostward* (Almeida).

Television credits include: *The Crown* (Netflix); *Doctors*, *The Game* and *Holby City* (BBC), *Coronation Street, Peak Practice, Trial & Retribution, Midsomer Murders, Prisoners' Wives* (ITV).

Carlie Diamond – Laura

Carlie Diamond trained at Bristol Old Vic Theatre School, graduating in 2022. This is her professional stage debut.

Anya Murphy – Anna

Anya trained at the Guildhall School of Music and Drama. Theatre credits include: *Rice* (UK tour); *Amsterdam* (UK tour). Television credit includes: *Eastenders*.

Hywel Simons – Harry

Theatre credits include: *Witness For the Prosecution* (County Hall); *Hay Fever* (Lyceum, Edinburgh and Glasgow Citizens); *Operation Black Antler* (Hydrocracker Theatre Company); *Noises Off, Three Sisters* (Colchester Mercury); *Enquirer, A Doll's House* (National Theatre of Scotland); *Betrayal* (Glasgow Citizens); *The Passion of Port Talbot* (National Theatre of Wales); *Red Bud* (Royal Court); *Money* (Shunt); *The Prime of Miss Jean Brodie* (Northampton Royal); *Dangerous Liasons, Romeo and Juliet* (New Vic); *Dracula* (UK tour); *Dancing at Lughnasa, The Rivals* (Exeter Northcott); *Double Indemnity* (Nottingham Playhouse); *Badfinger* (Swansea Grand); *Anna Karenina* (Plymouth Theatre Royal).

Television credits include: *Wolf, Dreamland, This Country*, Poldark, *Casualty, Celebrity Masterchef, The Passion, Casualty 1907, Little Britain, Heartbeat, People Like Us, The Bill* (series regular), *Score, The Flint Street Nativity, Roughnecks.* Film credit includes: *Enig.*

Holly Adomah – Marketing Consultant for WoLab

Holly Adomah is a theatre marketer based in South East London. She began her career as marketing intern at Park Theatre and eventually became the first and last marketing manager at The Bunker Theatre. Holly has led marketing campaigns, for instance the sold out *My White Best Friend*, for which she received the Social Media Presence and Activities OFFIE Award in 2020 for The Bunker and has worked for theatre venues and companies such as the Barbican, Shakespeare's Globe, National Theatre Productions, The Albany and Stratford East. Holly is also the founder of Holly's Angels, a volunteer food distribution service operating in theatre spaces to provide support to communities during the COVID-19 pandemic.

Jonathan Chan – Lighting Designer

Jonathan is a lighting designer and graduate of the Guildhall School of Music and Drama. His credits include: *The Solid Life of Sugar Water* (Orange Tree); *Heroin to Hero*, *Move Fast and Break Things* (Edinburgh Fringe); *Move Fast and Break Things* (Camden People's); *The Straw Chair* (Finborough); *Maybe Probably*, *Belvedere*, *Snowflakes* (Old Red Lion); *Different Owners at Sunrise* (The Roundhouse); *Don't Send Flowers* (White Bear); *Life of Olu* (Theatre Peckham and Golden Goose); *Fester* (Cockpit and Bridge House); *Barstools to Broadway*, *Amphibian* (King's Head); *Opera Scenes* (Bridewell); *Sticks and Stones*, *Time*, *Random* (Tristan Bates); *The Refuge* (Barons Court); *Urinetown: the Musical*, *Opera Makers* (Guildhall School); *Fidelio* (Glyndebourne – Assistant Lighting Designer); *Anna Karenina* (Guildhall School – Assistant Lighting Designer) and *Auricle R&D* (Guildhall – Associate Lighting Designer).

Daniel Denton – Projection Designer

Daniel Denton is a London-based visual artist and video designer. With a background in illustration and experimental film, he has created live visuals across theatre, opera, dance, fashion, broadcast and installation, and his video design work has garnered him multiple award nominations. Recent credits include: *Kinky Boots* (New Wolsey/ Queen's Theatre Hornchurch); *Happy Meal* (Traverse/Australian tour/ Brixton House); *Hedwig and the Angry Inch* (Leeds Playhouse/HOME

Manchester); *The Bone Sparrow* (York Theatre Royal/UK tour); *iGirl*, *On Raftery's Hill* (Abbey Theatre); *For the Grace of You Go I* (Theatre Clwyd); *Whitewash* (Soho Theatre); *Flashdance* (UK tour/South Korean tour); *Sketching* (Wilton's Music Hall); *Ready or Not* (Arcola Theatre/UK tour); *Misty* (Bush Theatre/Trafalgar Studios).

Nominations include: WhatsOnStage Award for Best Video Design (*Misty*); Broadway World UK Award for Best Video Design (*Happy Meal*); Off West End Award for Best Video Design (*Misty*, *Sketching*); Theatre and Technology Award for Creative Innovation in Video (*Ready or Not*).

Matt Eaton – Sound Designer

Matt is a sound designer and composer in theatre, film, sound art and games. He is an associate artist at Creation Theatre Company in Oxford.

Matt is an Off-West Award winner of Best Sound Design for Guildford Shakespeare Company's and Jermyn Street Theatre's *All's Well That Ends Well* (2020); composer and sound designer for Shasha and Taylor's *Everything I See I Swallow,* Edinburgh Fringe First winner 2019, and sound designer for Andrea Asaaf's *Eleven Reflections on September,* winner of Best Experimental Feature Film at the Silk Road Awards, Cannes in 2021. The film has numerous selections and awards worldwide. He is a founder of the musicians collective Pram, creators of cross-platform productions *Shadow Shows* (Edinburgh International Film Festival 2014); *The Photophonic Experiment* (Oxford Contemporary Music tour) and numerous album releases on the Domino Recording Company imprint.

Recent credits as sound designer include: *Pictures of Dorian Gray, The Massive Tragedy of Madame Bovary, All's Well That Ends Well* (Jermyn Street Theatre); *Brave New World* (Dir. Jonathan Holloway for Creation Theatre Company); *Furious Folly* (Mark Anderson's large scale artwork, commissioned by 14–18 NOW); *The History Boys* (UK tour); *The Time Machine* (London Library); *The Crucible* and *Orlando* (as artist in residence at the University of South Florida); *Pyar Actually* (for Rifco Arts). As composer credits include: *A Page of Madness* (Flatpack Film Festival 2019); *For-wards* (Birmingham, city-wide workshops in field recording, and commissioned work); *Nosferatu* (Warwick Arts Centre); *Faust* (Flatpack Film Festival 2017); *The Cabinet of Doctor Caligari* (Midlands Arts Centre); *The Picture of Dorian Gray* (London, Trafalgar

Studios). VW and British Telecom advertisements. Sound Art: *Everything Must Go* (Friction Arts, Birmingham); *Faith and Fracture* (York Minster); *Twelve Tones* (Ikon Eastside's city-wide project, Birmingham). Games: *Pool Panic* (Nintendo Video Game).

Frey Kwa Hawking – Dramaturg

Frey is a dramaturg and theatre critic who has worked with and read for theatres, companies and competitions including WoLab, the Bruntwood Prize, the Young Vic, the Bush Theatre, Sheffield Theatres, Free Hand, and the Women's Prize for Playwriting. He is an organising member of the Dramaturgs' Network and has trained through the Royal Court Theatre's Script Panel and Paines Plough/45North's Re:Assemble programme. He mostly writes for Exeunt Magazine, The Stage and WhatsOnStage.

Ingrid Hu – Set and Costume Designer

Ingrid Hu is an award-winning scenographer, designer and artist working in theatre and multidisciplinary design in the UK and internationally. With a focus on materiality, contextual and conceptual thinking, she creates spaces and environments that are alive and empowered to co-author, investigate, and respond to varied perspectives.

Recent credits include: *Mission* (The Big House); *The Global Playground* (Manchester International Festival and Theatre Rites); *Chotto Xenos* (Akram Khan, world tour); *Athena* and *a Kettle of Fish* (The Yard Theatre, London); *A Slightly Annoying Elephant* (Little Angel Theatre, London); *Light/Dark* (Uppsala, Sweden); *Curiouser* (UK/Norway tour); *Zeraffa Giraffa* (Little Angel Theatre and Clapham Omnibus Theatre, London); *We Raise Our Hands in the Sanctuary* (The Albany, London); *Hong Kong Impressions* (Yuen Long Theatre, Hong Kong); *1908 Body And Soul* (Jacksons Lane Theatre, London); and *You May!* (The Place, Arnolfini, UK; Onassis Culture Centre, Greece).

Awards include: 2014 Aesthetica Art Prize finalist (3D design and sculpture); 2011 D&AD Yellow Pencil Award (UK Pavilion, Heatherwick Studio); 1998 Neptune Theatre Blackmore Award, Canada; and 1996 Caran d'Arche Sunday Artist of the Year, Hong Kong.

Max Juan-Balch – Technical Stage Manager

Max has recently worked as a lighting designer for Italia Conti's 3rd Year Drama shows, lighting designer and technical coordinator for an Aerial Dance Show and assistant production manager for the spectacular for the Private Opening for Battersea Power Station. He has a Master's from Guildhall in Collaborative Theatre Production and Design, and works freelance across London.

Misha Levkov – Writer

Misha Levkov launches his playwriting career with *In the Net*; the first in a trilogy of plays (and a novel) on politics and private life in the unsettled present day. He has previously written books and essays on modern culture and literature, and has lectured on the subject around the world. All of his work concerns the mystery of modernity: how we struggle to live up to our moment and to break into a better future.

Vicky Moran – Director

Vicky is a theatre director based in London, working predominantly with new writing. She has worked with companies such as: Donmar Warehouse, Soho Theatre, Cardboard Citizens, The Pleasance, Kiln Theare, Clean Break and Theatre503. Vicky is currently working as a National Theatre Connections mentor director, an INNOVATE Project Associate at The Young Vic, and is one of the 2022/3 Artists in Residence at Arts Depot. Vicky is also the lead artist and director of women-led company, *In Her Strength*.

Website: *www.vickymoran.co.uk*

Nadia Sohawon – Movement Director

Nadia is an actress, choreographer, fire eater and martial artist born and raised in North London.

She started on the street dance scene early, learning locking and popping with London OG Jimmy Williams and Patrick Cesar, and then joined underground street dance crew Boy Blue in 2002, led by Kenrick Sandy MBE and producer Mikey J Asante. Boy Blue developed into a hip hop theatre company and went on to win an Olivier award for their alternative production of *The Pied Piper*.

In 2003 she founded freeYOURstyle Collective, which subsequently developed into a talent agency. Through the years, she has managed mainly POC and LGBTQ dancers from the underground/battle scene, working with artists such as Chaka Khan, Florence and the Machine, Dua Lipa, Ed Sheeran, along with other artists, and brands such as Gucci and Toyota, as well as an array of shows.

Nadia's choreography and dance contributions include: *After Life 2* (Netflix); *Rocketman* (Paramount); *2012 Olympic Opening Ceremony* (Boy Blue); *Alice Chater* (Virgin-EMI); *Dizzee Rascal*, *Alexander Wolfe*, *Mariah Carey*, *Diversity* (Limitless Tour); *Blaze* (Stage); *Catch Me Daddy* (Film 4); *Allstars* (Vertigo films) and more. Nadia also assisted Oscar winning director Danny Boyle on E.O.E., a dance film for BBC and won best choreography for short film *BOSS* at ALTFF Toronto. Nadia has also worked with award-winning theatre company Les Enfants Terribles, led by Oliver Lansley and James Seager, on plays *Bedtime Stories* and their latest work *United Queendom*, directed by Christa Harris.

Alistair Wilkinson – Creative Director for WoLab and Lead Producer

Alistair is a highly-experienced, award-winning, queer, working class and disabled artist, originally from Manchester, now living in East London. They trained at Royal Central School of Speech and Drama, as well as on The Royal Court's Invitation Writers Group, and also completed an MA at RADA/Birkbeck. In the past they have made work for organisations such as the BBC, Punchdrunk, Sky TV, The National Theatre, The Old Vic, Barbican Centre, Shoreditch Town Hall, Arcola Theatre and Curious Monkey, amongst many others. A lot of Alistair's work focuses on themes of grief, sickness, intimacy and intoxication. They are the former Head of Artist Development at The Old Vic and have just finished as Talent Development Lead at Punchdrunk, working in the UK, internationally and digitally. They are an Associate Artist at The National Youth Theatre, a Connect Artist for RTYDS, a Trustee for Boundless, and a Script Reader for The Bush Theatre, Theatre503, Theatre Uncut and The Papatango Prize. Alistair is the Founder and Creative Director of WoLab, and to date, they have raised over £1.8m in funding for various artistic projects.

WoLab

WoLab is a working laboratory for artists to create. They provide performance makers of all experiences with the opportunity to have a go. WoLab trains, mentors, nurtures and creatively entitles artists, helping them discover and refine their talents, and then showcases those talents to the industry. Recent work includes *ENG-ER-LAND* by Hannah Kumari, which so far has toured to 28 venues; *For a Palestinian* by Bilal Hasna and Aaron Kilercioglu, which enjoyed an acclaimed five-star sellout run at Camden People's Theatre and Bristol Old Vic, and *Rainer* by Max Wilkinson, which dazzled audiences last summer at London's Arcola Theatre.

Other work in development includes: *Screwdriver* by Eve Cowley and Elin Schofield; *A nightmare is witchwork* by Billie Collins; *A Romantic Comedy* by Tiwa Lade; *Tiger* by Tom Kelsey; *Hot Rain in Hackney* by Alistair Wilkinson. Past work includes: *First Commissions* (Paines Plough); *The Actor-Writer Programme* (Theatre N16/Bunker Theatre); *Man-Cub* (RADA/King's Head); *PlayList* (King's Head); *happy ever after?* (Bunker Theatre) and R&D's of *heavymetalsexyanimal* by Sam Rees (Theatre Deli) and *Asperger's Children* by Peter Machen (Trinity Laban).

Foreword

It's a long reach but a short step from grief inside a family to the wounded world. It's a different distance from voices in the writer's head to acting bodies who prance across a stage. Theatre covers the distance. Our private lives go public in their suffering and joy. The innermost sprites leave the brain to climb a net shamelessly.

Laura says to her father, 'People need to picture a better world.' 'I try,' Harry answers, awkwardly and honestly, 'I can't.' But – we do need to picture a better world. Which will only come to pass when we imagine it and make it real.

Theatre under threat to its survival should be the most ambitious theatre. It should be intimate and political, irritating and serene. It will never come easily because it lives inside the noisy family of collaboration. It comes from within to live without: it is in-sight out-cast.

Misha Levkov

Winner
**Fringe Theatre
of the Year**
2021

A small theatre with big stories

Jermyn Street Theatre is a hidden gem. It combines the comfort and convenience of the West End with the intimacy of a studio. Every seat has a perfect view of the stage, and even a whisper is audible. Every seat is a premium seat.

Our tiny bar offers a selection of soft and alcoholic refreshments.

Piccadilly Circus and Leicester Square are moments away, and the restaurants, galleries and bookshops of St James's are on our doorstep. This is a secret theatre in the heart of the West End – once found, never forgotten.

In 1994, Howard Jameson and Penny Horner discovered the space, and raised the money to convert it into a beautiful theatre. Since then we have staged hundreds of plays and musicals, winning countless awards. Many productions have transferred in London or to Broadway.

This is where careers ignite, where playwrights take risks, where great actors perform just feet away from the audience. This is where magic happens.

🐦 @JSTheatre
f @jermynstreettheatre
📷 @jermynstreettheatre

our friends

The Ariel Club

Richard Alexander
David Barnard
Martin Bishop
Katie Bradford
Nigel Britten
Christopher Brown
Donald Campbell
James Carroll
Ted Craig
Jeanette Culver
Valerie Dias
Shomit Dutta
Anthony Gabriel
Carol Gallagher
Roger Gaynham
Paul Guinery
Debbie Guthrie
Diana Halfnight
Julie Harries
Andrew Hughes
Margaret Karliner
David Lanch
Keith Macdonald
Vivien Macmillan-Smith
Kate & John Peck
Adrian Platt
A J P Powell
Oliver Prenn
Martin Sanderson
Nicholas Sansom
Andrew WG Savage
Nigel Silby
Bernard Silverman
Anthony Skyrme
Philip Somervail
Robert Swift
Paul Taylor
Gary Trimby
Ann White
Ian Williams
Marie Winckler
John Wise

The Miranda Club

Anonymous
Anthony Ashplant
Derek Baum
Geraldine Baxter
Gyles & Michèle Brandreth
Anthony Cardew
Tim Cribb
Sylvia de Bertodano
Janie Dee
Anne Dunlop
Robyn Durie
Maureen Elton
Nora Franglen
Robert & Pirjo Gardiner
Mary Godwin
Louise Greenberg
Ros & Alan Haigh
Phyllis Huvos
Frank Irish
Marta Kinally
Yvonne Koenig
Hilary King
Jane Mennie
Charles Paine
John & Terry Pearson
Iain Reid
Martin Shenfield
Carol Shephard-Blandy
Jenny Sheridan
Brian Smith
Frank Southern
Dana-Leigh Strauss
Mark Tantam
Brian & Esme Tyers
Jatinder Verma

Director's Circle

Anonymous
Michael & Gianni Alen-Buckley
Judith Burnley
Philip Carne MBE & Christine Carne
Jocelyn Abbey & Tom Carney
Colin Clark RIP
Lynette & Robert Craig
Flora Fraser
Charles Glanville & James Hogan
Crawford & Mary Harris
Judith Johnstone
Ros & Duncan McMillan
Leslie & Peter MacLeod-Miller
James L. Simon
Marjorie Simonds-Gooding
Peter Soros & Electra Toub
Melanie Vere Nicoll
Robert Westlake & Marit Mohn

In the Net

To seek joy in the saddest places. To pursue beauty to its lair.
(Arundhati Roy, The Bomb and I)

Characters

Laura Kovacs-Collins, *twenty-one*
Anna Gupta (*Laura's half-sister*), *twenty-seven*
Harry Ben Collins, *young fifties, father to Anna and Laura*
Hala Badri, *refugee from Syria, late thirty- early forty-ish*
Immigration Officer, *Young Sr.*
Councillor, *Felix Young*
Estate Agent, *Mr Tremaine*

The play is set during a twenty-four period 10–11 July, 2025. All subsequent productions should place the year two years in advance of the production year.

Act One

Scene One

A cluttered sitting room in Kentish Town: wood floors, high ceiling, tall curtained windows, worn furniture, including a shabby ample sofa, two pillowed chairs, a good-sized desk at the rear. Leaning back in one of the chairs, head thrown over an arm, **Laura** *draws on a sketching pad.* **Anna** *reads an account book at the desk.*

Laura   Are you even listening?

Anna   Of course, I'm listening. I heard every word.

Laura   Well, then?

Anna   Well then, what?

Laura (*leaning forward*)   Shall we sort it out? It's no use dreaming.

Anna   You mean the Eruv?

Laura   What else are we talking about? You say you're listening, but you're somewhere else. You're bored . . . I'm boring you.

Anna   It's not that. It's just –

Laura   Just what?

Anna   You're moving too fast.

Laura   *You're*! I thought we were in it together, *two* of us. Who saw things the same . . . *Whole* sisters, not half.

Anna (*going towards her*)   We do, we do. Absolutely! The two of us, inseparable again. Only –

Laura   Only what?

Anna   Only you're in the middle of everything. You need to *think*. (*Pause.*) You haven't finished mourning for your mum.

Pause, **Laura** *looking out window.*

Laura   I'm not *trying* to finish mourning, I'm in the thick of it . . . *You* had a mother; she died too. Didn't you want to keep the pain . . . if you couldn't keep her?

Anna   I loved your mum.

Laura   She loved your loving her . . . So why won't you make Eruv with me?

Anna   I'm only saying you should stay with your feeling, the main one, loving and remembering Miriam. You don't need anything in the way . . . I'm not saying no.

Laura   'Not saying no'. Is that what the Buddha taught?

Anna   I've stopped learning from the Buddha now. But yes. To think through everything.

Laura (*sharply*)   That's a way to think about nothing.

Laura *exits right,* **Anna** *left.* **Hala** *enters left, pulling buggy, sees no one, exits.* **Laura** *and* **Anna** *return (from opposite sides).*

Laura   I need to matter. We all do. Everything's falling apart.

Anna   Laura, Listen! You can't even say where you'll be next week.

Laura   Which is why we start now. (*Turning toward the audience.*) Look here. (*Gazing over our heads, speaking pensively.*) We go down from the roof of the shed, drop to the garden, and through the trees to the lane. (*Pointing.*) You can see it there: the plane tree with the low branch that reaches the postbox.

Anna (*looking out too*)   I see it. It's good, . . . But –

Laura (*turning away, angry again*)   *But*! Only always but. Who saved anyone with but – or changed a world? Who mourned or loved with but but but . . .

Anna   Yes *but*. Because you need to see through the sadness. It's a fog – being so sad.

Laura (*softly*)   It's true.

Anna   So what's the point of rushing out? And acting up.

Laura   Because we're late. It's the tenth of July, 2025. It's nearly midday. We were late before we started . . . Anna, people are drowning and the planet's burning. It's emergency for real and for us. Mum died. The least we can do is run to heal who's left.

Anna   I feel differently. I believe in things that move slowly – you know that.

Laura   *Don't I?*

Anna   Slowly. But you can't stop them. (*Looking up to see* **Hala** *entering pulling a small buggy with a heap of clothes.*) Also . . . – there's Hala.

Laura   Naturally there's Hala. But how can she be a problem?

Hala   Yes. How can Hala be a problem?

Laura (*turning*)   Sorry! I didn't see you.

Hala   I didn't mean to interrupt. You were saying, Anna?

Anna   I was only saying Laura should think how her knots and threads are going to stir a ruckus. (*Turning to face* **Laura**.) And it's even what you *want*, the noise – you've said as much.

Laura   Not a ruckus. No anger, definitely no violence. But yes, *blatant*. We're speaking up for people. Up and out. We're speaking with Hala.

Hala   I feel that Laura, I know how you care. (*Pause.*) But I only came to ask if you're sure about the clothes. (*Pushing the buggy forward.*) Miriam's dresses, her blue jumper, the Tartan scarf, these boots I never saw off her feet – (*Gesturing.*) all this.

Laura   I'm sure. My mother's dead: I'm sure of *that*. So you should take her clothes to anyone who needs them.

Anna   When we were small, we hid inside that dress.

Laura (*ignoring her*)   Giving the clothes to your friends is what she'd choose. But to you first, Hala. If they can be useful.

Hala   But we're all right, my friends and I. We've shared and traded. And if you make a good exchange, and cut and stitch, you end with more than when you started. We're all right . . . The clothes aren't for us. They're for the shelter on Leighton Road. I met some women there from Sheffield: they'd do well in these. If that's all right, Laura.

Laura (*surprised, adjusting*)   The shelter opposite the bakery? . . . From Sheffield? . . . You're right, my mum would be happy.

Hala   That's good then.

Laura   It will be strange though, won't it? To pass people on Leighton Road wearing the floppy hat she liked.

Anna   Good things shouldn't feel strange.

Laura   But that's not what philosophy says, not Hegel –

Anna   Enough, Laura.

Laura   Not for me. Hegel –

Anna *exits.* **Laura** *watches her go, then turns to face* **Hala**.

Hala   But Laura?

Laura   Yes?

Hala   You should have your Eruv. It's wrong to worry about me. I'm not a porcelain bird. I'm a teacher who lost her students . . . You called the Eruv a lane of safety.

Laura   It *is*. An avenue to the future.

Hala   You should have it then. Absolutely. But Laura? . . . what's an Eruv?

Laura   I told you.

Hala   You tried to tell me, but I got distracted by your bad Arabic.

A stirring at stage right, a door slams and **Harry** *enters with* **Estate Agent.** **Hala** *eases past with the carriage of clothes.*

Scene Two

Harry *moves into the room with the* **Estate Agent.** **Anna** *visible, standing aside, stage left.*

Laura   Papa.

Harry (*seeing the disorder*)   What's this? (*Then quickly.*) Oh yes, I do know. (*Turning.*) Here's Mr . . .

Agent   Tremaine.

Harry   Mr Tremaine's from Kubler and Martin, he's come to look at the flat. And Mr Tremaine, – excuse the state of the room . . . You don't have children, do you?

Agent   Lovely things children, they keep it churning, and there'd be no Kubler Martin without them. But children, I'm afraid, are not my line. Don't want and won't have them. (*Short pause and wink.*) I've *been* a child. (*Looking left and right.*) Not that you haven't done well. (*Turning.*) May I look around . . . and leave you to your things. (*Stage whisperly.*) I won't ask! (*Steps out right.*)

Laura (*glancing at* **Agent**'s *disappearing back*)   What's this about? Who's he really?

Harry   You must have known, Laura, that we'd have to sell the flat.

Laura   Why?

Harry   *Why?* . . . because the money isn't there. We have to let it go . . . As soon as possible really. (*Gesturing.*) Mr Tremaine –

Laura   From Kubler Martin.

Harry   – thinks –

Laura   It's giving in.

Harry   It's not giving in. There's no choice.

Laura   What happened to the money, Papa?

Harry   The bank slips went when your mother died. More than half . . . Money was never her point, but we had enough . . . People trusted she'd do the right thing, which she did . . . Which she tried to do.

Anna (*entering from left and keeping across stage from* **Laura**) What of *my* mum? Did people trust her too?

Harry   We were young. Your age. Younger. We thought money and children fell from trees . . . We had nothing and travelled India. But you know that.

Anna   I knew it, but I let it go in monastery . . . Now I'm here, it's coming back.

Harry   What?

Anna   I remember hearing 'Anna, Anna', and thinking momma was inside me, and I could only breathe because she was pumping my heart. She was the throbbing inside me.

Harry   Brinda was writing with the right hand and feeding you with the left. We thought we saw a way. I was for the drugs that cure, she was for the words.

Laura   It sounds another world.

Harry   The Madras story needs writing down, she said, you have to let people tell it. She walked tall in the streets.

Laura   But my mum –

Harry   Wrote nothing down. Too dangerous, also too slow.

Laura   She saw the Emergency coming . . . But she didn't know her dying was part of it. (*Pause.*) Why do your wives die?

Anna   Laura!

Harry   I think it's because they lived. (*Pause.*)

Agent (*poking head into the room, just to the side of* **Hala**)   You know about the cracks in the plaster and the fixtures in the lav?

Harry   Yes.

Agent   They'll have to be repaired before we show. Bad plumbing in dark places is *rogue*. Totally rogue. (*Head withdrawing.*)

Anna   Would my mum have been for Eruv? Would she have signed with your other daughter there, the wild one?

Harry   Laura's convincing . . . which she doesn't get from me. If you don't want Eruv, stay out of sight.

Hala *enters right, pulling an empty buggy.*

Hala   There's no avoiding Laura. And why would anyone try?

Laura *in reaction becomes more energetic with the twine, stretching across an angle in the room, wrapping it round a chair.*

Harry   There's room on the coast. Miles of hills. You'll have Eruv as big as a castle, and it will be safer there. Also (*Leaning toward* **Hala**.) you're that much closer to Syria.

The sisters exchange cringing looks.

Hala   But you *know* I'm not going with you. I stay with the others from Idlib. I've always said so. I keep with the ones whose wounds I know . . . and then later, you and I can meet – when I'm free and equal, not rare and precious.

Harry   But why shouldn't you come regardless? We'll have some money from the flat . . . And I haven't said! – My post came through this morning: with a pharmacy in Eastbourne. It won't be London, but London's not forever. And if the drought gets worse, it's good to be near water . . . (*To* **Anna**.) Have you kept to the ration?

Agent *is back in the sitting room, pacing, taking measurements, stepping over and around the yarn. The sisters turn away.*

Anna   There's enough for tea.

Hala   It's what we say in Idlib, 'Tea will be the last to go'.

Laura, *moving forward, pulls the twine so the* **Agent** *has to step awkwardly over it.* **Hala** *moves to the table and sits, watching the others.*

Laura   But we won't really leave, will we, Papa? You said, 'Only if necessary.'

Anna   *Laura.*

Laura   We can scrimp . . . or put a room out to rent. (*Pause.*) There's space now.

Harry   Stop, Laura! Everything's more expensive by the hour, and nobody knows how to manage the cold that's coming.

Laura   We'll find work, Anna and I. (*Pause.*) She'll be thinking, I'll be doing.

Anna (*putting a hand on her father's neck*)   We can figure something out.

Harry (*sighing*)   I feel there's a hole where life used to be . . . I need to talk to Miriam about Miriam dying.

Laura   It's wrong to leave now. Of all the times there's ever been, not now . . . It's running away.

Anna (*quietly, insistently*)   Let it be, Laura!

Laura *turns in frustration, goes to the window.* **Harry** *passes hands through hair, then looks to* **Hala**.

Harry   Tell me really, Is there any news? (**Agent**, *entering, passes alongside.*)

Hala (*ignoring the* **Agent**)   There's rumour. They say there'll be another tightening next week, so I need proof of identity always with me. I said, Do you mean my arms and legs? I brought them. I brought this swollen foot. I have my wound . . . and a picture of my son.

Agent (*calling from offstage*)   Master bedroom is magnificent, floors and ceilings to die for.

Harry (*to* **Hala**)   Can we make you more comfortable?

Hala   I'm comfortable enough . . . Today it's been almost daily life. I go to buy the day's pita and see the newsagent who smiles. The greengrocer says, 'Sunny this weekend.' I nod until I think they could take me away by Tuesday.

Laura (*from the window*)   We won't get daily life until we deserve it.

Harry   Why not just have it? Wake, work, have a meal, have a laugh. Miss your mum but *carry on*. Do the everyday.

Laura (*pacing nervously as she talks*)   You can't do the everyday, Papa, when the whole world's off a cliff, and your mother's dead . . . The usual's lovely. Your bad chemist jokes, and the floorboards creaking . . . But you can't not see! The dry earth's cracking when it's not drowning. They're pushing Syrians off the ledge, and people don't recognise themselves in the mirror.

Everyone falls silent. The **Agent** *stands still across the room for a moment.*

Harry (*turning to* **Hala**)   I only worry about –

Hala   My interview.

Harry   Yes.

Hala   I'll know something by evening . . . Or nothing . . . But it's all right! I'm all right. Warm enough, cool enough. Enough tea, enough women friends.

Silence.

Anna *has picked up twine and is pinning it against the top of the window. The* **Agent** *sneaks a look at her stretched-out body.* **Laura** *is sitting in the other window frame, gazing abstractedly into the room.*

Agent   I have what I need, thanks. Apologies for the tramp . . . I didn't hear *anything* . . . Did you see in the Standard? They called us 'parasites'. Well, with these gorgeous floors, I'm a happy parasite. And where would you flat-sellers be without us?

Harry *walks out with the* **Agent***, stage right.*

Scene Three

Hala*, coming forward, turns to* **Laura***, who sits cross-legged on the floor.*

Hala   And what's an Eruv? You were saying –

Laura   Eruv. (*Takes a breath, then goes on.*) It's an old ritual my mother liked, and it gave me an idea. So I went to the Borough and today's the day I see where we stand.

Hala   Where you stand? I still –

Laura   Well, you have rules on Sabbath.

Hala   I know.

Laura (*speaking quickly*)   And the Rabbis saw the rules can get too tight. So they invented Eruv – which is a place you choose where the rules don't hold, so you can do what's necessary – even when Sabbath says you can't. You make a rule to break your rules.

Anna (*to* **Hala***, still from a distance*)   It can sound like a scam, which is why I worry. A way to wriggle out of your promises. Go shopping on Sabbath.

Hala   If it seems that way – why isn't it that way?

Anna   It's what they always ask. It's what they'll ask Laura if she gets that far.

Laura 'Ask Laura?' Anna? Still keeping clear? Not for Eruv after all?

Anna I'm for *you*.

Laura (*briskly*)   Then you're for Eruv. (*Turning to* **Hala**.) It's deep when you think about it . . . We get a law, the Sabbath law, to rest – to rest and pray . . . if you pray. Anyway, to rest. But sometimes, you have to act. So we revise. We open the day, so we can move and do – because of Eruv.

Anna (*to* **Hala**)   That's the loophole.

Hala Loophole?

Anna An escape clause.

Laura *walking as she talks, draping twine over chairs and lamps.*

Laura If you need to think about it like that, then do. But I see it as a way to loosen the knots we tie on ourselves. Teaching ourselves how to change.

Hala Why have the rules at all? Why not wipe the slate clean and start fresh?

Hala *picks up a loose end of woollen cord and begins to move with it idly.*

Laura (*tone rising*)   But do you really want to be that creature who erases what's past and invents life out of thin air? Isn't the point – we come from *somewhere* and know what we want because we see where we've been?

Hala It's true. We come from somewhere . . . (*She thinks some more.*) Does it have to be a Jewish thing?

Laura It doesn't have to be. It happens to be. That's what Mum taught us. 'Speak from where you are. Don't wait.'

Hala But do you have to believe to make Eruv?

Laura (*quickly turning around*)   Who says so?

Anna   They all do. No one will take you seriously. They'll burn you, Jews and Gentiles both. Think, Laura! No Rabbi will take what you're giving. Which looks like nothing they've ever seen. And doesn't have to happen today.

Laura (*over her shoulder as she exits*)   Don't be a silly in-betweener, Anna. It will be Eruv like never before. It can wake people up to what's happening.

Scene Four

Anna *strolls from left, speaking into phone, walking as she talks.*

Anna   Yes . . . No . . . No.

I left before I was ready. It's true. But you knew I'd be leaving. You said I grieved too much for their suffering. I do.

Two beats.

Back in the world? – It's thrilling . . . it's awful.

You wouldn't recognise me. I eat everything.

Beat.

What do I want? I don't know. To be lost with the rest of them.

Two beats.

You're the one who taught it. My first week in monastery when you were teacher-mother. How the only way to find something is to be lost where it is.

Beat.

Are you sitting in the dip of the green stone? I picture the light off the hillside falling into the lake.

Two beats.

Not being ready is a way to get ready for something else.

I see new things. But through other people's eyes. (*Looking across stage at* **Laura**.)

My sister's.

Beat.

Laura . . . Laura Eruv-maker.

Act Two

Scene One

*The **Councillor** (Acting Deputy Chair) raps his gavel.*

Councillor   Our review of the water crisis resumes next meeting. Until then, the southeast keeps to seventy-five litres per. Vigilance all! We're only a borough in a city on an island near a continent. And if the rain won't come, the refugees will. Chaos is nobody's friend . . . Next item: proposal for an Eruv in Leighton Grove. Ms Kovacs, are you here on the tick of 2 p.m.?

Laura *bustles front. A screen shows Leighton Grove in Kentish Town.*

Laura   Here I am.

Councillor   We haven't met. Laura Celia Kovacs-Collins yes?

Laura   Yes, and you –

Councillor   Felix Young, councillor, solicitor, and as of this morning, Acting and Provisional Deputy Chair.

Laura   Honoured, Deputy Chair.

Councillor   Acting and Provisional.

Laura   Honoured, Acting and Provisional.

Councillor   So! . . . That's done. Will you begin?

Laura   You have the report, you have some photos, and on the easel, you have a map. It shows our Eruv running from Leighton Grove, east and south to Toriano, do you see? And then making a loop to the mews and back again. (*Pointing.*) Right here.

Councillor   Please. May we take seven steps back and three to the side? What's your aim and purpose, young lady?

Voice One   What does it mean anyway? An eruf? What's eruf, please?

Laura   Well, the report has it all.

Councillor   Can you give the highlights?

Laura   It's simple really, if you let it be. The Eruv's an area you mark. You map it with nylon, or wire, or thread, and inside your space on the Sabbath, you're exempt, you . . .

Councillor   Exempt? From what? Exempt how?

Laura   Let me say, and I'll tell you. Exempt from Sabbath rest. So inside the Eruv, you can work. You can carry.

Voice One   You're joking!

Laura   I'm not. Suppose you're in a chair, or suppose you need your buggy, or you have to get to shops or help someone who fell – you can. You can move through Eruv just as you please. It's free movement in there.

Voice Two   Why can't you do it anyway? You do it other days.

Laura   You can, you can. I can too. But Eruv does it differently. It's from long ago, not something you dream in a night. It's old, but it can change – which it should. Because we're alive *now*. And if you think about it – which is nearly all I do – Eruv can show how to be safe. And to resist what's false and brutal. Which is what everyone needs, no?

Councillor   I still don't see.

Laura   Did you even read what I wrote?

Voice One   We know about these Eruvs.

Laura   Eruvim.

Voice Two   We know what happened in Manchester, and in Hendon and Golders Green. We know about Teaneck and Tenafly in the States.

Councillor   What about them? What about Teaneck and Tenafly?

Voice Two   In Teaneck, the Eruv came, and the Orthodox came after. They moved in, priced up the houses, and sent their children to schools of their own. They pressured shopkeepers to close on Saturday. Let's call it what it is.

Laura   What's that?

Voice Two   A ghetto. A prison of your own making. And why do that again? . . . I'm a Jew myself. I'm proud, walking about. We don't need to close ourselves in, and tart ourselves up. Also . . . we don't need to rankle the Gentiles. Why insult them? Why get in their hair?

Laura   We don't see it that way. Not even slightly. It's actually the opposite of what we see. Do you know what the word means?

Councillor   What does it mean?

Laura   Eruv means 'mixture'.

Councillor   Mixture?

Laura (*insisting on the vision*)   It mixes home and not-home and sets you free. You gather with people and share bread in your net. It wraps you in – the nylon, and the yarn – and tangles you together. So it's a mixture.

Councillor   But still a Jewish mixture.

Laura   The Rabbis thought of it. But ours is a new Eruv for new times – in bad times. It's for anyone who wants to meet in the net . . . and think what to do next.

Councillor   Courtesy of Leighton Grove?

Laura   It has to come from somewhere. Mum taught us to go for goodness. To sing out, and to *go*. To join . . . So Eruv is Everyone, is what I think. It's for you too. Especially for you. You first.

Councillor   Well, yes, that's a point to dance with. It's all Hegel, yes? The one and the many. You have your thing, and you love your thing, so you call it everybody's thing.

Laura   If you like.

Councillor (*sarcastically*)   So we can fetch vegetables on your Sabbath? Push the buggy and not be struck down?

Laura   Fetch, or not fetch. It's up to anyone. Come along, do as you please. Bring the family. Take the piss. We don't care. That's the real mixture, us all mixed together. The pro- and anti- combined. It's the way to start living up to our lives. Stitching, weaving.

Voice One   I have to say, No thank you. Very much no thanks . . . Going along fine these days without a single Eruvim.

Laura *indicates more images of Eruv poles, blue nylon string.*

Laura   Do as you please. But think for a minute. It can be lovely inside a web, knitted in and wrapped around together. It's close and quiet. Also laughing and alive.

Councillor   Please. It's not hard to see things are bad. When the water goes, and the refugees come, you can't expect wussy blather from the Acting and Provisional. Everything's coming to a nub. Time to cut the wuss . . .

Scene Two

Austere office. **Hala**, *holding a black bag, sits at a slight angle to the* **Immigration Officer**, *with her hand on a folder in front of her.*

Hala   I've already answered that question. More than once.

Officer   Yes, I see you have, but we need to ask again.

Hala   Why?

Officer   To make sure you give the same answer.

Hala   What if it misses 'same' by only a little?

Officer   Then we ask three more times. And go from there . . . You see, we found an anomaly.

Hala   Anomaly? . . . Is that a weapon? A kind of gun? An anomaly?

Officer   It's something that looks like inconsistency. I'm sure you understand. If we're going to get anywhere, people have to be who they say they are.

Hala   I am who I say I am.

Officer   Yes, but it can't be for you to decide, can it now?

Hala   I'm not sure who better.

Officer   Please not to turn philosophical. We don't fancy philosophical. Now –

Pause as he looks into his screen.

Hala   May I look at my notes from last time?

Officer   We prefer not. We ask you to use the memory.

Hala   Some things are better forgotten.

Officer   You taught geometry in Syria.

Hala   I taught geometry in Idlib. Then geography. When the war came, the curriculum changed. Different shapes for frightened students.

Officer   What else did you teach?

Hala   Nothing else.

Officer   Nothing?

Hala   Politeness among the students; care for one another; humility . . . the emergency routes.

Officer   Now you're with *us*. It was a big day, we know, the night you entered the UK. Tell what happened.

Long pause.

Hala (*leaning forward, speaking softly*)   I came overland to Calais, where I waited a week to meet an agent.

Officer   The agent's name?

Hala   I knew him as Ahmed. It's the only name he gave. But he never arrived in Calais.

Officer   Do you know why?

Hala   Nobody knew what happened to Ahmed. We were told he wouldn't be coming. So I travelled with the others along the coast, to a spot where a man named Fernand had a boat. Seven of us crossed. We scattered at Folkestone. I don't know what became of the others. One –

Officer   Leave the others out of it. Tell what happened to you.

Hala   I rang Ms Kovacs. Miriam.

Officer   The records say you rang her from Calais.

Hala   I didn't ring her from Calais, I rang when we reached England.

Officer   Why did you say it was Calais?

Hala   I never said it was Calais. How could I? We were clear. I told her to wait, and I wouldn't connect until we crossed the border. Under no circumstances.

Officer   You told her? But Ms Kovacs was the one helping you. We know about that.

Hala   I taught her how to help. She listened, she knew how.

Officer   But the notes . . .

Hala   The notes are wrong. It's what I've told you and your colleague who was here. The tall one from last time. With the rude manner. You must know who I mean.

Officer   No one's trying to be rude. We're very careful. We want to do the right thing.

Hala   The decent thing?

Officer   The right thing. We have Ms Kovacs' phone, you see.

Hala   How did you get her phone? She's dead.

Officer   After she died, we found her husband. And explained our needs. Here it is (*He holds it up.*) . . . You can hear a message from the night of the fifteenth, the night you said you were in Calais.

He plays the message, which is in Arabic.

'*Your voice is fading, Mrs Kovacs. If you hear mine, then you know I'm in Calais. I cross at the arranged time tomorrow, but only if I'm well enough. My right leg, you see, is cut in three places. I can barely walk. I –*'

Hala   It's not my voice.

Officer   So you tell me. But you *would* tell me that. Did you hear what she was saying, whoever you say she is?

Hala   She's describing a wound in her right leg. She's in pain, you can hear the pain.

Officer   But when I look at your file, I see you hurt your right leg. You talked about infection, and a smell. It turned putrid, you said, while you waited in Calais. You didn't ask for a doctor. Why is that?

Hala   'Why is that?' You can ask? And where did you come from? Who let you in the country?

Officer   I was born here actually. Not that it matters.

Hala   I can't get a grip on what matters. Is that *anomaly*?

Scene Three

Return to the Council scene.

Councillor   Time to cut the wuss.

Laura   But not to decide without listening.

Voice Two   Do you mind my saying I find it sinister? You twine your smidgens past our bedrooms. Hocus-pocus shmooku. Which we don't believe but have to see. Those aren't your homes, or haven't you noticed? And who are *you* to tie your superstition to the jasmine on my gate?

Laura   But it's how you look at it! You call it sinister, but why not a chance to break the deadlock? It can make you think and help you feel. You see it as invasion, that's sad. Everyone has to try something . . . There's no standing still.

Councillor   Is it the solicitor in me? But I can't help wanting a bit of the humdrum around here. Just a tittle. Some fret over traffic calming or Sunday morning church bells. Do we really need an Eruv maven showing up with yarn in her head?

Laura   It's an exchange of gifts.

Voice Two   Christmas in Kentish Town.

Laura   If you like. There are different ways to say it.

Voice One   My way is to say, Thanks but not. Take your Eruv off, and go be a mixture by your Jewish selves. These are serious days. It's cat eat mouse out there. The streets get uglier all the time. Old men throw stones at children, and people in the shops are from who knows where. The smells alone . . . And instead of helping the drought, you tie the water in knots.

Laura   But really, how can an Eruv make more drought?

Voice One   You might harm a tree, or uproot a mains, if you go tampering and philootering.

Laura　I don't know philootering, but I know you're not being real or even slightly generous. It's healing not wounding. That can't be hard to see.

Councillor　Healing what?

Laura　Healing your bad temper for one, if you let it. The knots can show you a path. And an archway. And give a chance for defiance to get stronger.

Councillor　Defiance?

Laura　Of people with gavels.

Councillor (*handling the gavel*)　In fact, you can do a lot with a gavel in my gig and sector. It's a committee room around here, or haven't you noticed? Not an archway with curlicue. And who the tiff are you exactly? Kentish Town Eruv Action Group. Catchy name, but new to me.

Laura　Well. My mother, who died recently, told us about the weather – and the wounded. She could be fierce, too fierce for some. But you always saw how she wanted to keep people from hurt. She drove herself to death, if you want to know, and always pictured her work as small – 'as small as humanly possible, Laura'. She taught us to know people one at a time and see ourselves as nearly useless, but not quite.

Councillor　Do you get paid by the word, Missy? Or did you just forget the question? Eruv Action Group? Who are you?

Laura　As you see us.

Councillor　We see you . . . and the rest?

Laura　It's what my mother said: the longest step is from one to two. Everything gets shorter after that.

Scene Four

Hala *leaning forward on the table.*

Hala   I can't get a grip on what matters. You hear a recording on Miriam's phone, someone describes a wounded leg –

Officer   Right leg.

Hala   And I have a scar on my right leg. (*She raises leg, pulls up her skirt and shows a long scar above the right knee.*) So you conclude . . .

Officer   I conclude nothing. I inquire.

Hala   You inquire whether that scar is this scar, even though that voice isn't my voice.

Officer   Actually – we haven't settled that, have we?

Hala   I should know my own voice, shouldn't I?

Officer   We can't assume . . .

Hala (*voice rising*)   But can you listen? It's not my sound. Not even my dialect . . . It's not this person here, talking to you.

Officer   It's someone. She's there. With her leg.

Hala   And do you believe there's only one Syrian woman with a wound on her leg? That I'm the one and only, and you're going to catch me in a lie. I introduced Miriam to hundreds of us, everyone was broken somewhere, and now you find a dead woman's phone, and try to call me Anomaly.

Officer (*suddenly standing*)   We know it isn't you. Give us some credit, Madam, as people who play the tighter angles. (*Nodding at phone.*) It isn't you, but it might as well be.

Hala   Does someone else's pain make you happier to be alive?

Officer   It doesn't help to go into motives. We weigh each case by herself. Yours has some holes and corners.

Hala   Which is worse? The hole? . . . Or the corner?

Officer   Equally bad. Both level four. Right there with lying to Immigration.

Hala   Do you know? – I wouldn't treat someone this way in my classroom.

Officer   No?

Hala   Never.

Officer   What do you do instead?

Hala   First, no harm.

Officer   Is that something Arabic for something English?

Hala   I know what you can do to me – where you can send me.

Officer   Keep it in mind.

Hala   I keep to your rules and tick your boxes, because I tell myself, I have no power . . . Why do you need to make it worse?

Officer   We like it worse. It makes the others think twice. How many of you are there?

Hala   I count as one sitting here.

*The **Officer** wipes his face with handkerchief, offers it to **Hala**, who turns away.*

Officer   The heat's your element.

Hala   Don't misunderstand . . . We sweat too.

Officer   Would you like some water? Oh, *sorry*, (*Looking around.*) I don't have any. Seems your sandy shoes brought us the drought . . . Not enough room in the desert?

They look at one another for two beats.

Scene Five

Laura   The longest step is from one to two.

Councillor   I don't understand. Are you on your actual bloody own?

Laura   Anna hasn't said no (*Turning around.*), but yes, why not? I've been the one to start . . . because it came to me, when I was looking for it.

Voice One   Outrageous. Insufferable. Send her home to cradle. Get her the fuck out of here. Mud in the bath! Obscenity!

Councillor   Do you get a tickle from wasting committee time, young lady?

Laura   Never, and not at all. We all have to face the troubles by starting out and acting up . . . So it's good you're upset. We need to stop doing the usual. We need to meet in the Eruv and tie some new knots.

Voices One *and* **Two**   The worst yet. Apologise! Apologise!

Councillor   Nothing more to be said. Proposal fails to qualify. No work on a Kentish Town Eruv to commence or begin. Meeting adjourned.

The **Councillor** *strikes the gavel, and the scene shifts to immigration interview.*

Scene Six

Hala   Do you possibly think I'm lying? That my husband wasn't killed by a sniper in the market, and my son not kidnapped from his school? I wasn't raped by goons behind the station, and didn't get this wound from a twenty-year-old with a long knife? What else is on her phone, the dead lady?

Officer   I don't care whether you're lying. Not my call. I'm just the man with a fine-toothed comb.

Hala   A comb?

Officer   It's a metaphor, a figure of speech. It means look closely.

Hala   For the anomaly . . . Do you find it sexy?

Officer   What?

Hala   Wielding power over a woman, a refugee with a scar . . . with your fine-toothed comb?

Officer   That's out of order. And out of bounds . . . It can't help the case.

Hala   Which?

Officer   Being rude. Uncooperative. We're only trying to tidy a mess . . . And here's one more thing, please not to make it awkward: we need to redo the iris scan.

She looks at him but says nothing. He approaches her eye with scanning device, standing above her as she sits, carefully not touching her, but getting close, as we hear the sound of breathing, and then when finished, he pulls back suddenly.

Officer   I'll ping this to the lab in Bedford.

The **Immigration Officer** *moves to exit. He puts his paraphernalia in a small neat case – his signature (like the alarm clock in Peter Pan).* **Hala** *strides stage left, overtaking him to exit first.*

End of Act Two.

Act Three

Scene One

Anna *sits cross-legged on chair, body still, eyes gazing downward, as* **Laura** *enters stage right. She doesn't see* **Anna** *at first.*

Laura Were you doing Buddhism?

Anna Doing Buddhism? (*Uncrossing her legs.*) Reverse actually. I'm doing 'back to the world'. (*Glancing over.*) Are you angry after Council?

Laura Bruised like a peach . . . Embarrassed to be stopped by an Acting and Provisional Deputy Chair who wouldn't know Eruv if it tied his toes to his ears.

Anna It hurts, I'm sure it hurts. But it gives some breathing space.

Laura If that's what you think we need when the world's exploding.

Anna (*quietly*) I care too. We both care. There's more than one way.

Laura How many?

Anna There's my way . . . which says that we're nothing more than specks in the night. And it doesn't make me care less. Maybe more.

Laura I'm not a speck.

Anna Yes, you are, and I love you for it.

Laura And even if we are, we have to help. We have to find the other specks, until we make a cloud together.

Anna We do. But we can look at ourselves from far away. We can make the ego so small it almost disappears.

Laura I need my ego. I need it to care.

Anna   Maybe. Maybe. But if you could be more gentle with yourself –

Laura   Keeping-it-inside Anna.

Anna   Jumping-off-the-ledge Laura.

Laura   You're tall for a speck.

Anna   You're not.

They pause, feeling the mood shift, getting more serious, **Laura** *searching* **Anna***'s face.*

Laura   Really, wasn't it yesterday Mum was alive, Hala came, and it wasn't so hot? We were teasing Papa, learning Arabic.

Anna   I'm frightened.

Laura   Not you too.

Anna   Everyone should be.

Laura   Then why aren't they?

Anna   It's what I thought in monastery. How we're standing in sand and sinking up to our neck. Only the head's left, watching the sea rise . . . I know how it feels. (*Shudders.*)

Laura   Don't.

Anna   Don't what?

Laura   Don't make me lose my balance.

Anna   I wouldn't. I want the opposite.

Laura   Because it flips when I blink. I go to Uni to collect posters and a dozen friends sign on to rally. The next minute, water's draining from the mains, they say no to Eruv, and the rogues come after Hala . . . Is the world glowy and green, or did it turn to shit when we weren't looking?

Anna   Words aren't good for questions like that.

Long silence. **Anna** *moves right.* **Laura** *steps after her, then stops.*

Laura   Where are you going? It's dark out there.

Anna   I need to walk.

Laura   Always going somewhere.

Anna (*moving right*)   Always coming back to you.

Laura *exits left, chewing her finger in thought.* **Anna** *briefly exits right, but then circles back phone in hand, talking.*

Scene Two

Harry *enters left.*

Laura   Papa. You're here. But where's Hala?

Harry   She wrote to say she'd be home by nine. Her friends will bring her.

Laura   It's past nine.

Harry   It's been a long day . . . I heard the news about your Eruv. I saw our Deputy Chair. I'm sorry.

Laura   Don't be.

Harry   It was bound to happen. Eruv's a ball of yarn to most people.

Laura   To me too . . . It's how you weave it.

Harry   The Rabbi, did you hear, said you made a mockery of the law, which is ancient and sacred.

Laura   Mockery's not what we're about, you know that.

Harry   And it's not what Eastbourne's about . . . You need to persuade Hala. We have to get away from here. I know woods where you can walk all day and see no one.

Laura   That's not it, Papa! It's too late to leave, everything's coming down.

Harry   In a net?

Laura   People are kinder in the Eruv. Safety, food, taking the piss . . . Easing hurt. Going for the future. Everyone's invited.

Harry   Stop, Laura.

Laura (*turning away*)   I can't bear it.

Harry   We need to get past the pain.

Laura   I don't agree. There's no running away, not from Mum, not from the Emergency. There's mourning, and learning from Hala, and pitching in. Sharing chocolate. Caring for one another. Really caring.

Harry   Why do you call it 'Emergency'?

Laura   Well, you see, Papa, it's because it's an *Emergency*. What else do you call it when people seal the border like it's their wife's body? Or, when they need to find water, steal from someone's pail?

Harry   I know it's bad.

Laura   If you say it like that, you *don't*.

Harry   It's bad. But how can Eruv make a difference?

Laura   People need to picture a better world.

Harry   I try, I can't.

Laura   People need to inspire each other. Eruv means mixture.

Harry   Yes, you said . . . We buried her, Laura.

Laura   I didn't.

Harry   It's been six weeks.

Laura   It was yesterday . . . It's right now.

Harry (*standing*)   You ask too much of people.

Laura   Not enough . . . Mum wasn't right about everything. But she knew you have to throw yourself in, if you want to count. Really throw yourself. You have to bring your whole life with you. Including your mother who's dead.

Harry (*standing, exasperated*)   We need to stop with the daydreams. They're as bad as nightmares.

Laura, *sitting silent, as* **Harry** *moves left.*

Laura   Now where are *you* going?

Harry   I promised to fix the hinge on the bathroom window.

Laura   You should have promised to keep the house.

Harry   Your mother would have agreed with me.

Laura   How do you know?

Harry *exits left.*

Scene Three

Laura *throws herself into an armchair. Silent, looking around, then speaks.*

Laura   It's how it is. But what can it even mean to live without you?

You sat *there*. I lie on the floor. You're thinking, 'Settle, Laura', but never say it. You let me fret and call me Flutter.

This room, with the people and colours – the yowl and clatter of it! Thirty, fifty women. *More*. Talking, laughing. But when I needed, I could find your eyes. Because you knew I'd be looking.

I want to catch you in Eruv and nestle in the threads, the two of us and Anna. Hala if she thinks it's right. I know a corner where you could never die.

That last midnight when you said you were terrified and happy.

Laura *lies quiet for a minute, and then there comes the sound of a door rattling followed by a knock. She rises.*

Scene Four

Agent (*calling from the audience*)   Hello. Hello in there! Late I know, but us agents never sleep.

Laura (*mock cradling her ear*)   We sleep . . . when you let us.

Agent   You'll forgive when you know. We have someone getting keen. This could actually be it, and – can you hear me?

Laura   We hear you.

Agent   There's a market out there, you know.

Laura   Is there really?

Agent   So I need to make sure, can I say it nicely, that we don't have your knitting on show in the morning? Don't get me wrong. It's dainty work, really prim and frilly, and you carry it off so well. But – can I come up?

Laura   You can't come up.

Agent   It's just, clients are *modernista*. If you know what I mean. Even with your lovely old pile in Kentish Town, they expect the dust swept and tiles spiff. Nobody wants to hear about a hundred years ago. Fishmonger from Krakow this, pedlar from Odessa that . . . And one more thing.

Laura   I was sure there'd be.

Agent   When they ask about the cost of heating . . . tell them it's bad everywhere. And smile.

Laura *sits again.*

Scene Five

Hala *enters stage left.* **Laura** *scrambles out of the chair to stand and go to her, reaching out to clasp hands.*

Laura   Hala! Sit down. (*Moving chair toward her.*)

Hala   I'd rather stand, I need to collect myself.

Laura   Was it terrible?

Hala   They don't want me here. Is that terrible? I don't know.

Laura   Will you have something? There's enough for another tea.

Hala   Nothing . . . (*Looking around.*) Where's Anna?

Laura   Walking in the dark.

Hala, *after all, sits in armchair.* **Laura** *starts to talk then stops. They stay quiet. Then* **Laura** *can't help herself.*

Laura   I picture you in front of them. I can't stand it.

Hala   Don't let it happen to you.

Laura (*stepping back in sorrow*)   Does anything help?

Pause.

Do you believe in anything, Hala?

Hala   It's a stiff question.

Laura   If it's too personal . . .

Hala   It's not that. We've come to know each other quickly, and . . . everything's personal anyway.

Laura   That's how I think. Anna –

Hala   Still, it's stiff. 'Do I believe anything?' The honest truth is I tried to believe it *all*, which seemed the only chance. When I saw my husband's broken body, I thought, 'What if there's nothing but that? Flesh on a table with fat in the guts.' When I watched him die, I thought I'd try any faith I could.

Laura   Can you do that, though? Try someone else's? Can it get a grip on your heart?

Hala   Maybe not. Since I've been hurt, I think about the strangeness of people's beliefs and take what I can. Like a raven. Then I do the one thing I know.

Laura   Which is?

Hala   Teach your students the truth they can't deny. It's why I picked geometry – where you see the proof before your eyes. In Idlib, they say a teacher should be a surgeon: cut fast, then stitch together.

Laura   Do you think you can teach me?

Hala   You'd be a hard case, Laura.

Laura   Why?

Hala   You want so much that's good, but you only see with two eyes.

Laura   I read philosophy at Uni.

Hala   We know. But philosophy can't tell you how it feels to be someone else.

Noises left of footsteps coming down stairs.

Harry (*calling from off stage*)   Laura!

Hala   Apologies, but not your father right now. I don't want to have to say I'm all right.

Hala *quickly steps into shadows stage left, still visible to audience.*

Laura   I understand . . . I think I do . . . Papa!

Harry   It's hard work, the grit on the windowsills. Funny how you only notice things when you leave them.

Laura   Not *very* funny.

As he starts to move left, **Laura** *turns him right, glancing to* **Hala***, who is tiptoeing back to get her bag.*

Laura (*urging her father to rear*)   Over here, Papa.

He drops his 'scraper' and as he retrieves it and stands, he sees **Hala**, *who's been quietly exiting left. She turns toward him.*

Harry   Hala, you're back. When did you –

Hala   Only a minute ago. I was with the others. I –

Harry   But have you eaten? You must be exhausted.

Hala   It shakes you.

Hala *sits in the armchair.*

Harry (*to* **Hala**)   They rang for you earlier. I said, 'I don't know, I can't help.' They said they'd ring again.

Hala   There's no difference . . . Answering. Not answering.

Harry   But –

Hala   They'll find me when they please. They sniff you out.

Harry   There has to be a way –

Hala   – Miriam might have known.

Harry   I'm not Miriam, and I have to keep at the ceilings . . . But Hala –

Hala   Don't worry. It's not your struggle. You have your own.

Harry   I need to find the step ladder (*Hesitating, turning back, then moves to exit left.*) . . . I don't make much of a patriarch, Laura.

Laura   You don't need to stretch higher, Papa. Just come down to your own size.

Harry *exits.* **Laura** *looks over at* **Hala**.

Laura   Anna thinks I go too fast.

Hala You don't know enough, Laura. You know how to care for pain, and how to speak to the pricks. But it's only a start.

Laura Am I noisy and atrocious?

Hala It's the best of you. We depend on your beating wings. (*Smiling.*) And the chirp of your hope.

Laura You're mocking me.

Hala A bit. Because I have the right, and you haven't felt as much as you think.

Laura You make me ashamed.

Hala You make yourself.

Laura I'm ashamed, because I long for my mother, but you lost as much . . . And you suffered more.

Hala It's not something you measure.

Laura But the bastards hurt you.

Hala If they could, they'd hurt you too.

Laura I seem more sure than I am.

Hala You don't have it 'sussed', Laura. That's all. You shouldn't think you have it, just because you mean well.

Laura I don't. I –

Clatter at door and **Anna** *enters.* **Laura** *moves across stage.*

Anna Hala!

Hala Can we talk? When you've had a chance to settle?

Anna Now is good.

Harry *enters.*

Harry I thought I heard the door. Where were you?

Anna I was walking. To the gardens past our old school. It brought me back.

Laura (*from across the room*)   It was hard when you were gone to monastery.

Harry   Now you're here.

Anna   I'm between. It's the place where I can help . . . Between here and somewhere else.

Laura   Is that where you were in the dark?

Anna   I saw someone in Joshua Lane when I crossed the road.

Harry   Was it Tremaine?

Anna   Tremaine?

Harry   The agent. Laura says he came earlier.

Anna   No, not him. I'd know that one anywhere. If anyone needs the Buddha . . .

Hala   Anna?

Anna   Yes, let's go upstairs.

Laura   No, you stay here. Papa's at work on the ceiling, and I'll tidy our corner . . . (*Leaving the room.*) Under protest.

Scene Six

Hala *sits,* **Anna** *keeps standing.*

Anna   Do they even listen to what you say?

Hala   They ask what I want in England. I say, to gather what's left of my family. To gather *myself*. To heal, to teach. To notice dignity when I pass a mirror.

Anna   They don't let themselves hear.

Hala   They squeeze you in their vise, and use the truth against you. Which they find funny.

Anna   But they have to admit –

Hala   They admit nothing. They keep you thirsty, so your mouth's too dry to speak English.

Anna   It's good you're strong.

Hala   Why do I have to be, Anna? . . . Don't tell a desperate person she's strong. Don't go thinking it helps . . . If she was strong once, she's not now. Not after fear wears her down, and she feels embarrassed for no reason.

Anna   It's true. I'm idiot.

Hala   I won't be petted. 'Good refugee, lie down in detention. Drink your curdled milk.'

Anna   I know . . . I don't know.

From opposite wings, **Harry** *calls to* **Laura** *who opens eyes and replies.*

Harry   Laurie! . . . Laur!

Laura   Over here, Papa.

Harry   Will you help me find –

Laura   If I can.

Harry   – the socket and ratchet kit? In the red case.

Laura   Mum had it last.

Laura *and* **Harry** *withdraw, left and right.*

Hala   Laura won't admit her mother could fail.

Anna   Anyone can fail.

Hala   Her plan put us into the Channel too early that night. If we hadn't realised, the French would have found us at the next tide.

Anna   She must have been mortified. Miriam –

Hala   She was. But who would blame her? She tried even when she was dying.

Anna   No one knows how to die.

Laura *reappearing right.*

Laura   I found the kit.

Harry (*appearing*)   Where was it?

Laura   Under the hats and brollies.

Harry *and* **Laura** *withdraw.*

Hala   My son rang this morning. He'll be fourteen next month. 'Do you still hurt?' he said. My mother wept on the line.

Anna   I – how do you bear it?

Hala   There's no secret. There's bearing it – or not.

Anna   It's suffering.

Hala   In the middle of missing my husband, I think about being cut, then my mother and son, my student – and all this. What *is* it?

Anna   It's suffering. It's Kentish Town and it's flooding in Pakistan, because bread's too expensive in Egypt, and girls are sold in Thailand. Ask Laura.

Hala   I used to live with ordinary things. Now my brain –

Anna (*slowly, hesitantly*)   Sometimes, if you empty the mind by watching it. . .

Hala   I tried to empty it. I tried to try. But anger stayed in there.

Anna   Everyone has to find a way. For me, it's seeing myself from the end of the universe.

Hala   So many will die this winter. I'd pray it won't be Waddah – but I don't pray.

Anna   Sometimes people pray without knowing it's what they're doing. They hear themselves say things that come from nowhere.

Hala   I won't lose my voice, even if all the rest goes.

Anna   Miriam would shout with you from the rafters.

Hala   Now Laura will. And what I came to say –

Hala's *phone rings. She fetches it from her bag, puts it on the table, looks at the number, then at* **Anna***, shaking her head. Declines call.*

Hala (*concentrating again*)   What I came to say –

Anna   Yes?

Hala   Laura's right, is what I wanted to say. It's no good creeping along. Obedience makes it worse.

Anna   I know.

Hala   If you cringe, they kick harder.

Anna   It feels impossible to find a way. But –

Hala   Laura's right about making noise and throwing confusion in their eyes. Making a net so everyone has to notice.

Anna   She's right, but –

Hala   But?

Anna   She wants to be for everybody, and also for her mum. It's too much.

Hala   These days I don't know 'too much'. Nothing's enough, is more how it seems.

Anna   I don't –

Hala   It's not enough to *know*.

Anna   It helps.

Hala   Yes, but also to wave your hands and sing. To show more of us than they can count. Otherwise they pick you off one at a time.

Anna   You sound like her.

Hala (*smiling*)   Not like you?

Anna   I'll be there. Without fail. I'll be there. But –

Hala   But?

Anna   But I'm for breathing out, not just breathing in. Someone has to think how it will be afterwards.

Hala   She leans on you.

Anna   That's all right. It lets me lean back.

Pause.

Hala   There are things I can only say to you: Laura and I are too alike to talk.

Anna   That's all right too.

Hala   The best students think they're already teachers.

Sharp knocking comes from off stage.

Anna   I won't answer.

Hala   They have no right – unless Harry gives permission.

They sit uneasily.

Anna   Talk to me. Tell me something.

Hala   What?

Anna   Anything. (*Looking around.*) Your first memory.

Hala   My first memory? (*She half-rises cautiously, looks around.*) I was sitting on the floor in the kitchen – my mother standing over me. Cooking. Some beans fell off the counter and scattered on the floor. I chased them under the cupboard and put them in a red bowl. My mother thanked me. 'You have them all,' she said. I counted them. Sun came through a crack at the top of the door.

More knocking on the door. They look at one another.

Anna   You said you were always maths, but –

Hala   I was a maths bird. Because I was shy, I think. It gave me someplace. Hala, maths. My brothers used to show me off on the football pitch. What's three sixteen and one two five over seven dot nine?

Anna   What is it?

Hala   It doesn't matter. It let me be . . . Childhood was all right. Even the beginning of the Civil War was all right. We didn't call it Civil War then.

Anna   It's what we say in monastery. How life seems like life, until one day you cross the line.

Hala   They killed my husband, but we stayed three more years.

Anna   Because leaving home –

Hala   It's more than that. It's leaving the person you are. Who can choose it? The others looked to me, I was surprised, I didn't pretend to know. But I decided.

Louder knocking.

Anna   (*softly, as if to herself*)   It's so fucked.

Hala   I haven't been alone since I found my way out.

Anna   They want you unsettled. The more flummoxed the better.

Hala   'Flummoxed?'

Anna   Baffled. Flustered.

Hala   I try to remember how 'fucked' they are.

Anna   You have to see them and see through them.

Hala   It's that or go under. I was daughter and sister, then teacher. But they press you back. Even after you leave, they have a thousand ways to squeeze you. Even the ones who help, even Miriam –

Anna   I don't know how to help except to stand here.

Hala   That's something.

Anna   It's late.

Pause.

Anna   I think they've gone away.

Hala *and* **Anna** *move to stage left. As they reach exit,* **Laura** *appears on the right, carrying a candle, walking to centre then turning back.* **Anna** *sees her and follows.*

Scene Seven

Laura *notices* **Anna** *and turns around. They look at one another and speak from a distance.*

Laura   Do you know? . . .

Anna   What?

Laura   It's hard to say.

Anna   What?

Laura   Even more than Mum sometimes, you were the megastar. The only one who liked when I went too far.

Anna   It let me hide in the shadows. And I like moon best.

Laura   I like high noon.

Anna   You *do*, and I love that in you.

Laura   Then why won't you say you're with me?

Anna   *But why is saying it best*? 'I'm with you! I'm with you!' Isn't it better how when you look up, I turn out to be there. It's a quiet thing.

Laura   I won't be quiet.

Anna   No.

Laura   I believe in speaking out so they retaliate. Which lets me swear 'You *fucker*!' and they come back 'Double fucker,' and I go, '*That's* original! . . .' and when they're still wondering whether they can call you bitch, you step on their toes.

Anna   I still like my way.

Laura   Which is . . .

Anna   Sussing it to the hilt. Knowing what they weigh, so you can hit the pressure points, and they shrivel . . . It can be done with stillness.

Laura   As long as it's serious, (*Smiling.*) *seriously playful*.

Anna   I agree. It's Buddha. It's breaking through by knowing how. Miriam was nearly Buddhist.

Laura   Mum? She spent her time being Jew / not-Jew. It got exhausting – even though she was right. She taught me to be impure, and I thought it meant sex. (*Laughs.*) But she meant life. Impure life. Crossing the lines because they were lines.

Anna   It's what our dad said in the old days: 'Walk till they stop you'.

Laura   But we're the ones now. And it's what you used to like: planning it out, making it happen. Do you still?

Pause.

Anna   I see it, Laura. Eruv.

Laura   I was sure you did.

Anna   It needs to be surprising. It puts everyone on stage. And once you're in, you have to think about what's best . . . in the order of what matters.

Laura   Eruv like never before.

Anna   Part Buddha.

Laura   But still Eruv . . . And surprising because people think they already know. Blah blah the burning planet. Blah blah blah the people drowning in the sea.

Anna (*quietly*)   Suffering.

Laura   You hack away at the cave walls. Show what's possible.

Anna (*looking at audience*)   You surprise people into being better than they are.

Stage goes to shadow. **Harry** *crosses front, moving a sofa slightly, straightening a curtain with exaggerated shake. Then exits left.* **Anna** *follows.* **Laura** *walks to right, trailing nylon that she winds around a chair. Exits.* **Hala** *comes forward from rear and looks out through the window.*

End Act Three.

Interval.

Act Four

Scene One

Exterior: simple tree and fence, physical or painted, real ladder. For half a minute or so, **Laura** *and* **Anna** *work busily on the Eruv, putting just a few framing cords in place.*

Anna   Pull tight and move a bit to the left. (*They adjust the cord, tugging from opposite sides.*) Good.

Laura   It's starting.

Anna   Not so difficult, if the tie is tight.

Laura (*stepping back to look*)   The next bit's harder. I'm not sure how to get out of the shed to the lamppost. It has to make a doorway from the kitchen to the garden, as if you never left the house.

Anna   Best not try it in one go, better to make two doors, one from shed to drainpipe and then from pipe to post. You can meet the fence at the corner.

They work in silence; then **Anna** *drops from above and surveys the work and* **Laura**.

Anna   Think how your mum would be feeling.

Laura   Haven't I, though? . . . She'd be in the crux of it . . . up in the trees, stretching out her thin arms, holding nothing back. Seeing it my way finally: making something to see something.

Anna   She'd see it, and she'd have us singing. Something from *Gigi* or Piaf.

Laura   Except she's dead.

Anna   There's that. But . . .

Laura   Don't try to make something good out of it.

Anna   I won't. You're right. I only meant . . . you're not dead.

Laura   Not in the slightest. It's my whole idea. Not to be dead in the slightest . . . And to make Eruv with you . . . No matter what they say.

Anna   I see how to do the left turning. But not the reach across the drive. The poles have nothing to grip. We need another strut. Reach! There.

Laura *can't quite reach, so* **Anna** *takes the cord higher.*

Laura   I don't feel you're taller. I know you think so.

The two sidle right, looking up, thinking. **Laura** *gives the ball of cord to* **Anna** *and then steps backward, unspooling her end, lifting it above her head and nearly colliding with* **Hala***, who has a circle of rope on her shoulder. They embrace.*

Laura   Are you here for Eruv, Hala?

Hala   Yes, exactly. You put the idea in my head, Laura. How could a teacher resist? The geometry! (*She walks around the netting.*) My friend Qamar, rising architect, you know him – he studied the design and saw a mosque through your Eruv. We look at something in a new way. And thank you.

Laura   Do you mean to join? because yes, of course, absolutely. The more hands the better . . . More geometry.

Hala   We decided it fit us to start here. With you, alongside you. Our Eruv. Near, but not the same.

Laura   Hala, are you joking? Don't tease. You know this comes from a deep place.

Hala   Ours is deep too. We come to plant something that grows from *us*. Where we are . . . here and in London. Far from home but needing home. We make it to show it.

Laura   Are you making, though? Aren't you really taking?

Anna (*stepping forward and between*)   But it's always taking, isn't it, Laura? No making without taking.

Laura   Who says that?

Anna   I say it. Aren't you taking from your mother?

Laura   Yes. Of course. I take from Mum, always from Mum, but not her alone. It's a winding road. Through a desert to a green field. It's across Hungary, Poland, France. It has a story.

Anna   But it can change. You're changing it already. Threading it the way you see it.

Laura   With you.

Anna   Yes, with me. But it's what you told them: Nobody owns Eruv . . . Look at you, Laura. You have no permission, no right. You heard them yesterday: they don't want your nylon in the jasmine. You don't care, and good on you! But it's not any Eruv the old Rabbis would know . . . not to mention Rabbi Yalom, who thinks you're mad.

Hala   We call ours Eruv too. You said it meant mixture. We're mixing. We're mixing it up with you.

Laura   My mum saved you!

*Silence, then **Hala**'s deliberate speech.*

Hala   Miriam and I, we were on our way to friendship . . . which could have been. We were each too proud . . . but there might have been a way . . . And now, I make Eruv. Alongside and here.

Laura (*stiffly*)   But really how can you?

Hala   We can. We can because we think it's right and good to take and make. From you and with you. We knew it wouldn't be easy, Laura. But we're sure it's worth the pain.

Laura   And the point? Of the pain?

Hala   Honestly?

Laura   Honestly.

Hala   It's a way to be equal. Side by side. Your Eruv and ours.

Laura   It's not a game, two players on the pitch . . . Eruv should mean change. It matters if you let it.

Hala   It matters. We see it like you, only from our angle and story. And you're right again: no good to wait till they find you, best to meet them where you are. It's how we see it too: the coliseum out the kitchen door.

Hala *begins to stretch and tie some thread.*

Laura   But –

Hala   Does it knot or does it ravel? . . . Do you furl the strands, or thread without a cut? . . . And – and when you enter, how many come at once? I mean in the Eruv as you see it, Laura.

Laura   I don't own Eruv, nobody does. But it's a specific thing. You can walk in my Eruv, Hala, whenever you please, most honoured guest. But it's narrow and nasty to thieve it for yourself.

Anna   Don't say that, Laura.

Laura   I see so much, don't you? In sanctuary and brass. It's what Eruv should always have been, if only it knew. A place where we can be for each other, defending the weakest . . . and being defended when we're least. Until we're ready. Then brass.

Hala   For us, it's a nervous place, the Eruv. Which is good. It stays disorderly . . . unquiet. It lets you see what's hiding when you think you know it all.

Laura   That's a good thing. But it's different.

Laura *and* **Hala,** *side by side, ignoring one another, working at the same pole.* **Laura** *pulls sharply at her cord,* **Hala** *pulls back on hers, and as* **Laura** *refuses to move, she loses balance and falls. Her eyes fill with some tears.*

Laura   Oootch.

Anna   Are you hurt?

Laura   Not enough.

Hala (*half teasing*)   I thought Eruv was safety.

They stand awkwardly near. Then **Laura** *abruptly climbs back up and makes a next stitch, while* **Hala** *turns to hers.*

Hala   Will you pass the hammer?

Which **Anna** *does, leaning forward, and as a piece of cord dangles from* **Hala**'s *frame,* **Anna** *catches it and begins working with her, which* **Laura** *notices from above.*

Laura   It's not right, Anna.

Anna   What's not right?

Laura   Leaving me. I don't like being left, I thought you knew.

Anna   I haven't left *anyone*, especially not you. I'm just here, helping Hala.

Laura   Are you thinking how it looks?

Anna   To who?

Laura   Aren't we sisters?

They carry on working in the Eruv, **Laura** *climbing back to lower right, and* **Hala** *looks down from above left, with* **Anna** *between the two. After a silence,* **Hala** *speaks.*

Hala   Miriam didn't save me, Laura. I saved myself.

Hala *exits right.*

Scene Two

Councillor Felix Young *arrives stage left.*

Councillor   Excuse me, excuse me . . . *excuse* me. Is this what I think it is?

Anna   What do you think it is?

Councillor   Exactly which was discussed yesterday, exactly which was not approved. Your, what d'ye call it? Eretz? Made of string, and hair, and other people's property. Looks *like* it. We thought you mightn't be listening . . . I didn't just happen to stroll by. We need it down.

Anna   We?

Councillor   Department of Environment, Access, Safety. Sub-committee on Planning. Us.

Laura (*coming out of her upset*)   What's unsafe here?

Councillor   It's not you're unsafe . . . though you probably are. The team's been reading up on your Erun today.

Laura   Really? And what did you learn?

Councillor   Well, for one thing, it's not a proper one, is it?

Laura (*glancing toward* **Hala**'s *work*) Which do you mean? Which one isn't a proper one?

Councillor   You have to make agreement – isn't that how it goes? You have to agree on the rental. With the local authority . . . With *us*, to put it bluntly.

Laura   Actually, you're right about that. It's in the teaching. To make Eruv, you sign a deed. Nominal rent, peppercorn. Couple of quid.

Councillor   Which you haven't done.

Anna   No time like the present. Will you take two pounds?

Councillor   I can't do that. I'm not here to negotiate.

Hala *enters left.*

Hala   What are you here for then?

Councillor   To unstring Contraption. (*Stepping closer.*) Or take it down in one go.

Hala   Take what down?

Councillor   Your . . . Eruv.

Hala   But there's no Eruv. I heard what you said. No Eruv without a deed from the Borough . . . There's no Eruv here. How ever did you think so?

Councillor   Please, let's be civil. Call me Felix. Let's untie some knots and talk over coffee. We can meet at the bureau on the High Street. I'm always there.

Laura   In fact, what's to take down? The trees and post are in our garden. Truly, we infringe on nothing . . . not even in this doorway to the bird feeder.

Councillor   Doorway?

Laura   You're right. It's only a doorway if it's an Eruv. Now we know it's not. Now it's a frolic among friends . . . A lark with some yarn.

Councillor   But if your ribbon can make a doorway, what's to stop sunbeams from being a window? –

Laura   Eruv in the head? Don't worry, we want it real . . . You'll know it when you see it.

Councillor   Already I see a tree limb climbing over the wall. You'll need to return it to your side.

Anna   But it's always grown like that. It's not our doing, it's the way of the tree.

Councillor (*busying with the limb*)   It's past time for some tidier angles in the neighbourhood. Your Eruv will have contributed after all . . . So let's stay easy. And obedient. I have to insist, it's how I *help*.

He strains to lift the tree limb.

Hala   Absurd. It's hardly more than three feet past the line. Let it grow. It's a *tree*.

Councillor   Absurd to you. (*Still lifting.*) But everything's nicer when things stay in their place.

He exits stage right, as the three women look at one another in exasperation. But no sooner is he gone than he returns.

Councillor   There's something else. Food. You have to share your meal, am I right? It's what internet says. 'Food in Eruv exchanged and shared. Private goes public when you feed grapes to your neighbour'. Am I right?

Laura   You know it all. You have us cornered. We haven't agreed to share food in the Eruv . . . What Eruv?

Hala   Share with me anyway, Laura. Do you have something?

Laura   Only some figs. A few figs and nuts. The reds from Aleppo.

Hala   My gift to you. Share . . . as our agreement together.

Hala passes a fig to **Laura**, *who takes it, give her some nuts, and half-smiles.*

Councillor   You *people*. Won't you ever stop? . . . See you in council.

Exits right. The three women face the audience, sharing and eating figs and nuts, picking at stray branches and yarn. **Anna** *points left warningly.* **Hala** *nods to the two and steps back for safety.*

Scene Three

From above, looking through a window (could be window frame on a ladder), **Harry** *leans out then turns away. He can be seen puttering and fretting. Then leaning further out, he speaks.*

Harry   Anna? Laurie?

The two continue working on the net.

Anna   Dad.

Harry   Are you sure about this?

Anna (*pulling at a length of rope*)   It's not important to be sure.

Laura (*talking over her shoulder*)   Don't worry, Papa. It only makes you tired.

Harry   I didn't know you could get this tired without trying . . . It's like lying under a mountain. Who put it there?

Anna (*pausing and looking up*)   Losing love can put you under.

Harry   It makes me feel ancient and geezer.

Laura   Nobody wishes so well as you, Papa.

Harry   It hurts . . . your saying it like that.

Laura   It's only – sometimes a father should just watch his rebel daughters. And trot along after.

Harry (*receding into window*)   I do. I should . . . I'm not used to myself.

Anna   You used to climb. I remember, you held the branch with both hands, swinging . . . like you believed in God.

Scene Four

Sitting in front of their rudimentary Eruv, **Anna** *and* **Laura** *look up at him.*

Anna   I pity him, I wish I didn't. He's too young a father to be pulling at his fingers . . .

Laura   He was happy as long as Mum had us on simmer. He knew what to do. He could care.

Anna   At monastery, I pictured you three here . . . and wondered why I wasn't.

Laura   Has it been all right though, Anna? Being home and that?

Anna   If your mum had to die, I had to hold and let go. It's the adoptee's love . . . you don't know how strong it gets. When she went, it made me think of everyone she knew – and us in the middle.

Laura   Still taking care of everyone?

Anna   If only.

Laura   Nothing calling you west?

Anna   I miss the feeling of seeing, really seeing. . . But I chose. When you're there, everything gets clear but far away, even your own hand.

As they talk, they rock back and place feet against feet, increasingly affectionately close.

Laura   Is it like a castle?

Anna   It's like a garden.

Laura   A garden . . . You guided the pilgrims, you said. And helped them clear their heads.

Anna   If I could. If they could.

Laura   Everyone must have longed to keep you. I can picture their grip on your wrist.

Anna   I had to decide. Any further, it was losing my name, losing everyone's. Yours too.

Laura   Don't.

Anna   I didn't. It was a long road –

Laura   Three years.

Anna   Nearly four. But it's over. My life's in the hold-all, and I'm a free woman.

Laura   Nothing clasping tight in Devon?

Anna   Not a thing.

Laura   Not even, what was he? Eric? Or Derek? Snake in the garden.

Anna   Twisted double schmuck!

Laura   When did *you* get filthy-mouthed? Did the Buddha teach you?

Anna   Derek, the fucker. He preyed on the pilgrims until I packed him off. Nothing to say for himself . . .

Pause.

Unlike you.

Laura   *Mum* had everything to say . . . and said it twice.

Anna   She could say 'fucker' if she had to.

Laura   I was twenty, Anna, twenty, and not ready. I had plans for Mum and me, and . . . – I'm sorry! What am I saying?

Anna   Don't be sorry.

Laura   But you weren't five when yours . . .

Anna   Now look at us. Motherless.

Laura   Sisterful.

Scene Five

From stage right comes the **Immigration Officer**.

Officer   I'm looking for Hala Badri.

Anna   Sorry. Who?

Officer   Chala Badri . . . Recent arrival.

Anna   What makes you think she'd be here?

Officer   Our team put her here, give or take a lamppost.

Laura Your team? Can they do that, your team? Track her to a lamppost? And a hedge?

Officer Not much of a squeeze these days. Not with the geo-markers, and where your refugees are concerned . . . Not here then? I won't ask when she left, or how far she can get on the gimpy leg.

Laura Really, we don't know where a Badri could be. Lovely name, though. Should be a person attached . . . Look around. We have nothing to hide.

Officer In the meantime, would you know her sponsor? – Who would be a, a Gupta . . . an Anna . . . Gupta.

Anna (*looking out from above*)   I'm an Anna Gupta.

Officer You're Gupta, but we have you unmarried, with your father as Collins, Harry Ben Collins. (*Strokes chin.*) So how are you Gupta?

Anna I decide to be Gupta, as my mother was. It's how it goes with names. You must have one yourself.

Officer Let it be. You're Anna Gupta, and you're the sponsor, since . . .

Anna . . . since my stepmother died. Yes, I'm sponsor now.

Officer Yes, well, I came to say the iris scans don't square up . . . Nothing fatal, but biometric is biometric.

Laura *Is it?* Is biometric biometric? I hadn't heard. Had you, Anna? Does that *mean* something? . . . And by the way, is it language you use over there, I mean in the office you come from?

Officer I don't have your name. Now, I see I should. It's . . .

Laura It's Laura Celia Kovacs-Collins. I'm another who keeps cropping up.

Officer   Laura Celia, yes. We have you on the dial – with
your prints. You're the one with Eruv, yes? But that's neither
here nor there.

Laura   Not here anyway.

Officer   So it's simple-dimple for your Mediterranean
friend. Tell her, won't you? The iris in Bedford doesn't
match Kentish Town.

Anna   Which means . . .

Officer   It may mean nothing. But I'm sure you
understand why we have to be punctilious.

Laura   *Punctilious*! Don't talk to the man, Anna. There's
something wrong with his tongue.

Officer   I'll ignore the feisty one. But you do see, don't you,
how we have to run all the gamuts? HQ needs to be certain
that Person A stays Person A and doesn't turn into Person B.
So we'll be needing more tests and measures.

Anna   Such as?

Officer   We go back to the retina, and then the usual: voice
recognition, elbow reflex. We have numbers from
Southampton for the other quotients: skin moisture and
elasticity, face pattern, fecal integrity.

Laura   You're not serious . . .

Officer (*tone hardening*)   Not serious? . . . Easy for you to
caress your tidy little Eruv virtue and say, let them all in. But
picture what it means, won't you? They'll eat your
strawberries and sleep in your bed. You'll say, Oh, he's my
lover. But soon they'll lock you out the house. Add it up, and
subtract happiness.

Laura   We're not asking for every but *many* – many more
than one person with two irises.

Anna   You can't be doubting she is who she is.

Officer   Not doubting. Probing, sifting, sampling.

Laura   I was there, face to face to face, when my mother brought her home. No one's hiding under the skin. Hala is Person A. And Person A is Hala.

Officer   Stranger things have happened. You understand.

Laura   I don't.

Officer   For you, she's a person . . . with a name. And a smell. But why in blue begat should we trust her? Or you with the Eruv hair? Things change in the shadows. A person takes another name. And the iris? It could be telltale. What colour are her eyes? Do you even know?

Laura   What about your machines? What colour are *they*? Does machine A ever turn to machine B – and everything goes to crap?

Officer   No need to get excited. I'm only asking our Gupta sponsor to pass along word to la Badri. Who should contact us. Hala has our number and should ring as soon as possible. Not later than midday.

Exits right as **Anna**, *standing in the space of* **Hala**'s *Eruv, marked by fallen yarn, and* **Laura**, *standing, in her own, pick up and tie some knots.*

Scene Six

Hala *seen writing at window above the Eruv,* **Harry** *standing down below and calling up.*

Harry   Hala!

Hala   Is that you, Harry?

Harry   Not disturbing you, am I?

Hala   Not exactly . . . But –

Harry   I'm worried about the girls (**Hala** *turns to the table.*) . . . It can't be wrong, can it? To care about the people you love.

Hala (*trying to turn away*)   Is worry the way?

Harry   Do you know a better one?

Hala   You can be with them – all the way with them – even when you're not.

Harry   Who for you? Now, I mean.

Hala   My mother, my son.

Pause.

My son.

Harry   *Wad*dah.

Hala   Wad*dah*. He failed his last exams, but won't talk about it. Not to my mother, not to me. He only says exams won't matter when he leaves Syria. Failing's better.

Harry   You want to shelter him, don't you? When they're vulnerable, you spread your arms to cover them.

Hala   I do. But now – (**Harry** *steps closer and looks up.*) I need to cover my papers with ink. The height of my son, and weight of my mother. Where I was born. Where my husband died. And my signature, written a hundred times, as if they're hoping I'll spell it wrong.

She turns to the papers and tilts her body away from him. They're silent for a moment.

Harry   Do you know? –

Hala   What?

Harry   You wouldn't need so many forms if you came to the coast.

Hala   No?

Harry   You wouldn't need the housing papers, which Miriam said were horrible.

Hala   I can't ask any more from you, Harry –

Harry   Of course you can. It's what caring means.

Hala   And I don't *want* any more. I've been your guest. I've had as much as a guest should hope for. I'm a stranger, you were kind.

Harry   *Let* me be kind. Kindness can never be too much.

Hala   It can be.

Harry   Because I – because you deserve kindness and care. And shelter. No one should be thrown to those wolves.

Hala   It's a beautiful and difficult thing, host and guest. But it's time for me to be with friends. Not hosts.

Harry   We'll have space for you in Eastbourne. I've made sure. I have photos. (*Holding one up.*) A room of your own. Close enough, if something scares you.

Hala (*turning back to the desk*)   These papers are a nuisance, but my friends will help. If the police leave me alone, I'll be in Blackheath until a flat comes through.

Harry   Can you come down to talk a bit?

Hala   I can't. Not now. (*Looking back up and out.*) And Harry –

Harry   Yes?

Hala   It's not easy for a guest to say 'Enough'.

Harry   Take your time.

Hala   What you can give, you've given. You don't need to feel guilty.

Harry   No I –

Hala   You haven't hurt me. You didn't kill my husband. You –

Harry   No, of course not.

Hala   Do you need me to be grateful? I'm sorry, but it's burnt out of me – gratitude. But I can care about you as a decent bloke with persuasive daughters. Who are the best kind.

Harry   I don't need you to be grateful. I don't need anything. Except, I don't know, consideration.

Hala   I'm glad we met, but leave me be, Harry. Find Anna.

Harry   I like to be useful.

Hala   I don't forget people who grieved with me.

Pause.

But I need to get back to this heap – for my mother and Waddah.

Harry   There must be things you want –

Hala   I want things, everyone does, but not anything you have.

She draws back from the window. He stares for a minute, then withdraws.

End Act Four.

Act Five

Scene One

Scene opens on elaborate full-blown cat's-cradle of an Eruv, filling the stage, webbed and framed, intricate as a hedge, with hand- and foot-holds for ascending, descending, and hidden platforms allowing actors to move quickly in the netting.

Laura (*high in the lattice, waving and bowing*) Can you do this?

Hala (*boisterously leaning back*) It's easy. Look!

Laura But that's not it. You need to throw your head back and stand on one leg.

Hala And sing while you do it.

Laura I don't see you, Anna.

Anna (*visible from across stage and lower*) Over here! I'm reaching.

Hala Hold tight . . . Pull up.

Anna Thanks.

Anna *and* **Hala** *lean back, as on a trapeze.* **Laura** *burrows into the thick of it.*

Laura What can you see?

Hala Just Eruv, but who could want more? It's lovely in here.

Laura Your bit turned out so well, Hala, such clever turning to the sun.

Hala Which bit? I thought that was yours.

Laura Will you pass the nylon, Anna? I have an idea.

Laura *perches visibly in the net, while* **Councillor Young** *approaches from stage left.*

Councillor   I see you went ahead. Regardless.

Laura   Regardless, Councillor. But not thoughtless, or careless . . . Borough guidelines good, Eruv better . . . It even has a beauty, yes?

Councillor   It has a look, I give you that. Have a photo before you take it down. Share it with your people. Facebook. Or Fuck-a-gram.

Laura *swinging down to stand with him.*

Laura   Listen . . . We know we're irritating, which is half the point. But not the main thing . . . Underneath and inside, don't you hear something? Like an egg breaking open. An Eruv no one's seen before . . . You think it's insolent and flip. What if it has to be that way to open your eyes.

Councillor   I find it insolent and flip. And skanky and fucked. You didn't even ask the Rabbi. And my brother, Young Senior, who sweeps rubbish from the border . . . you don't want to *know* what he thinks!

Laura   Everyone's fussed, which is how we tell it's working. Here you are, and welcome. All in the net together, assembled and alive.

Councillor   In the net? Is that a come-on?

Laura   Won't you try? You don't have to call it Eruv.

She reaches for his elbow, but he pulls away hard.

Councillor   Do you know, I'm a reasonable man. Even in footie, I know you have two sides. So I keep my anger down because what's the point of hammering the shiny dickheads? End of the day, they flounce to poofdom.

Laura   Good policy.

Councillor   So it makes me wonder why I'm so red-pissed at you. I could hurt . . . your Eruv. You say, Make Eruv new. I say, How dare you shit on the borough? What a shabby way to mourn for your mother! Your dear mother who died.

Laura   And how dare you, Mr Acting Provisional Deputy!
How dare you tell me how to mourn for Mum. We mourn,
and make it new. Can you stop us? We say, It's too hot . . .
and time to heal the wounded who came in small boats.
Starting somewhere like here.

Councillor   You make it out of your heads, and poach a
name, when all you want is drama and cheap thrills. It's
children's diddly.

*She moves to slap him, but he ducks and turns away from the
glancing blow.*

Laura   Did I do that? Did I slap the Acting and Provisional?
I apologise . . . and I don't. You don't own the borough, or
the air between us. We want to make *you* new . . . Or do I
have to slap you again?

Councillor *pushes her to one side, steps in and through the Eruv,
separating strands to exit stage rear. Then he returns, sticking head
back through the net, looking up.*

Councillor   We have our eye on your water, you know.

Anna   Yes? Why?

Councillor   Drought-breaking mamas, aren't you? I see it
in your eyes.

Anna   Not a chance. We follow the rota to the letter. And
give back what's left at the end of day.

Councillor   Then you should know your ration's been cut.
Down to forty *per* in the area.

Laura   Which area?

Councillor   Eruv district. That area.

Laura   We never had to have drought. Not like this.

Councillor   You can't bounce what has to be, little missy.

Councillor'*s head recedes behind the Eruv.*

Laura (*unseen*)   Bounce.

Scene Two

The three are suspended in the net, at different levels, heads visible, as they watch him exit left, **Anna** *between the two others.*

Laura   Did I go too far?

Anna (*teasing*)   Laura too far?

Laura   You see how they hate you. They reek with it. They –

Anna   Enough, Laura. You got us here. Brava! Let's think.

Laura   Rosa Luxembourg says . . .

Hala   Let her think, Laura.

Laura   But it's not about us. We're only seeds –

Anna   Laura!

Hala   Don't let's squabble now.

Laura   No squabbling. Not when it's so gorgeous above.

Anna   When they get close, we more than show it. We flaunt it.

Hala   Because they think refugees run from them. But we don't. We walk, and then turn round.

Anna   We need to stay here –

Hala   . . . because where would we go? They find us when they want us. I'm talking in a net with sisters, singing to the birds. But on their screen I'm a spot of light . . . blinking.

Anna   When the siren goes, we scatter through the trellis to the higher rungs.

Laura   Clever, Anna.

Anna   So you move this way, Hala. Where there's more shadow. And Laura one step down and to the left.

They take steps to secure their positions.

Laura It can save water.

Hala A net?

Anna Because Eruv makes you careful.

Hala It does. Careful . . . and reckless for yourself.

Giving a bounce and twist.

Laura Do we call you sister, Hala?

Hala Call me Hala. You say it nicely now – your Arabic's better every day. Look at you!

Anna I'd like to see us from a thousand miles up.

Hala Better than the hooded ones below.

Anna Who look like weasels.

Hala It's how they bend their necks. More like turtles.

Laura They think, I'll pinch those cheeks and go to pub and pinch some more.

Hala When they come close, aim for the iris . . .

Pause.

But don't let's be grim. It's Eruv.

Anna Have a fig. (*Eating one, extending bag.*)

Hala With a red nut. (*They eat a bit from the bags.*)

Laura Save the rest. They can be useful if you know your reds. We'll teach the others.

Hala Who else is in?

Anna Kate, and the mates. Hanadi with theirs. And Geeta . . . Jack – and Tildy with her rogue guides, who promise to bring knots no one's heard of yet.

Hala When?

Laura As soon as they hear it's happening down at Eruv.

Anna   People sense the endgame. It's something you smell really.

Scene Three

From stage right comes the **Immigration Officer** *who looks up into the Eruv, peering.*

Officer   Brother Councillor tells me you don't play nice with your hands, Ms Laura . . . Which means everything ratchets up now . . . You didn't expect it to ratchet down, did you? . . . (*Two beats.*) Mrs Badri!

Officer *turns to address the audience, then pivots to look up.*

We know she's there . . . Bearing good news from Headquarters, Ms Hala! The bios came clean, and you turn out to match yourself after all. Just a patch of lab confusion: someone mislaid an iris . . . Tupper's chuffed . . . Always a pleasure to find a 'fugee who's one and the same. Everything forgiven . . .

Tries to settle his footing, looking down before looking back up.

You only need to clamber down, and touch your chin to the thermion. Hardly notice . . . if you're quiet with the needle. We'll have you clocked by dark, and I'm your Charlie.

Two beats.

(*Voice rising.*) We do need to meet now. Now meaning *now.* Otherwise, it's Code Mauve and Grade Seven . . . No One Wants That.

You ought to know better, Badri. Or haven't you heard? – It never does to bite the hand that slaps you . . . Remember, luv, just because you're clean doesn't mean you're not dirty . . . Nothing's over. It never is.

Exits left.

Scene Four

The three come out and stand in front of the net.

Anna   Are you all right? Hala? Laura?

Hala   Too angry to be afraid . . . They're no better than the ones who came with chains.

Laura   People can be beetles.

Anna   Or butterflies.

Hala   Someone should run for Hanadi.

Laura   I'll go.

As she moves to leave, they hear the sound of machinery dragged along pavement.

Anna   No.

They leap back into the cover of the net, climbing quickly, as the officer reappears.

Scene Five

Laura *sticks her head cautiously through the netting and is spotted by the* **Officer**, *who steps forward.*

Officer   You think it's good fun, local sport. You hide, we seek, tea-time giggles, cost-free. But it's girls like you who get on my particular wick. Airy-fairy, castles in the sky . . . What do you call it? Eruv-ism?

With rising menace, facing the audience, talking to **Laura** *over his shoulder.*

Officer   They never guess, the clever ones, how the State gets serious at end of day. A little this, a little that, you think we do dialogue forever? I say, What *is* this? You say, 'It's our Eruv'. . . . Give me a bleeding break! Brother Felix should have slapped your impudent phiz. We're not so . . . how should I say? . . . Fore-holding in my branch . . . *Call her here*!

No sound, apart from flutter in the netting as he steps forward to pull a strand.

This comes down like catkin. I'll be back. Five minutes . . . No, three.

Exits right.

Scene Six

Laura *climbs far into the net, and for a minute, we see signs of movement and a shaking of the twine. Some books drop to the ground, two loaves of bread, and three nuts, and a pole falls clanking at the side – but no speech and the stage stays empty.*

A siren goes off, rising for ten seconds.

Harry *enters, looks up but all are hidden.*

Harry   Are you there? It's important. They went through your room. I tried to stop them, but they held me in the chair, the blue one. A hink took your clothes. I asked, *What right*! – But they said you have no rights, no matter what the iris. Whatever that means . . . If you're there, tell me you're there.

Anna   We're there.

Harry   Don't move. Keep out of sight, but listen. The flat sold; it came fast at the end. Cash in hand . . . It was the Canadian – only we need to be out immediately . . . Well, the middle of next week, which is all right, because I've let them know on the coast . . . Can you hear?

Laura   Yes.

Harry   It's the right and beautiful thing. The hills are white. Under the sun, you can't tell hills from clouds. You have (*Beat.*) the sea. We need the sea . . . It's time to look after ourselves. Away from this (*Beat.*) tangle.

Anna   And Hala?

Harry   Of course, Hala. Everyone needs to be safe.

Anna   And her cousins?

The Eruv ripples to suggest the movement of many people hiding in the net.

Harry   How many cousins?

Anna   We haven't counted.

Harry   Let me meet them, we can discuss . . . Will you come down? – So we can talk? (*Looking around.*) All clear.

Anna   We can't come down, Dadder.

Hala   You come up.

Harry   In there?

Hala   Throw yourself in.

Harry   But how can that help? They know where you are; I told you. They can *find* you. (*He pulls at a strand.*)

Anna   Do you think they won't find you on the Downs? The drones know your footprints before you make them. There's no hiding.

Harry (*addressing the net in front of him*)   Maybe not. But there's getting through the day. And the next one, stringing life out. We read, we cook, we tease the neighbours. The hum of the everyday . . . What else is there?

Laura   There's Eruv. Time to take it seriously: it's about going in, making the wrangle *here*, not running to the coast. There's no *outside*! Wasn't that Mum's lesson?

Harry   I missed that one, I only saw her dying.

Laura   I saw it too, Papa. But it's not wrong to be alive. Someone has to be.

Harry *puts a foot on the netting to rise one step, and stays there. Through the next scene, he stands immobile, head bowed into the Eruv, not responding to the dialogue.*

Scene Seven

Sirens wail, then abruptly stop – **Officer** *enters, looks around, exits,* **Anna** *enters from other side,* **Harry** *still suspended at his first step up.*

Hala   It's closer.

Anna   I can see them around the corner.

Laura (*impatiently from within*)   Come up . . . Quickly!

Anna   Breathe.

Hala   We're breathing.

Anna   Because we need to change on the inside too.

Laura   Do you mean me?

Anna   I mean everyone.

Laura   Which changes first? Inside or outside?

Anna   There's no first.

Clatter from off. She exits. Empty stage.

Scene Eight

Laura   Anna's right. Breathing helps.

Harry (*still at his first step, looking up*)   But it feels like a game, Laurie. Like the games you played before you knew.

Laura   It's the net we live in, Papa, big and light and noodly, so you have to notice. Everyone likes Eruv once they know. Our friends are coming – pretty soon, it will be Eruv all over England.

Harry   But what then? What's it for?

Laura   We gather round, we eat and tell, and see other Eruvim on hillsides. Refugees have their choice of net, and some host picnics for the locals. We get a sight of how it will be after the drought . . . After the drought is over.

Harry   It's a lot to imagine from some knots and strands.

Pause.

I'm only being practical.

Laura   You're the best loved, dead-tired practical father. Who spawned Eruv children who can't stop now. But practical's not enough. It doesn't catch the vision.

Harry   Which is?

Laura (*standing tall*)   Which is knowing there's no escape – so rising high, kicking against cruelty, and singing for the light.

Hala   Come up. We can talk about everything.

Harry *looks right and left, starts to climb, slips, tries another place, sways with the rope, and then burrows cautiously into the netting, finally making it through, waggling his feet behind him.*

Scene Nine

The growing 'crowd' is seen to shift and move and clatter on stage left and stage right. **Anna** *leans forward to throw cording to a 'cut-out', some of it reaching the live audience in their seats.*

Anna   Welcome, and also thanks. We need your knitting too.

Then she turns back to look toward **Laura** *and* **Hala** *– only* **Laura** *visible at first.*

Laura   Can you see me breathing?

Anna   I see the light in your hair.

Hala (*appearing with length of rope*)   Hold on to the end of this, Anna? While I pull tight.

Anna   I have it.

Hala   I'm slipping.

Anna   Reach.

Hala   Wait! I found a rung.

Laura   One's always there.

Anna   Are you settled?

Hala   Kindled . . . It's good this high.

Laura   I feel taller.

Hala   Is that a yellow moon beyond the clouds? Or the white sun?

Laura   Looking down on merry Eruv jugglers, who keep the stars in their sky.

Hala   Because sometimes you find yourself somewhere. The shadows change, and you think life might be possible.

Anna   Hala!

Hala (*with relish*)   I could feast on everything I hoped for. The dead would come back alive.

Laura   Mothers and all.

Anna   It's solemn –

Laura   And playful.

She shakes a strand.

Hala   But you're right, Laura.

Laura   Right?

Hala   Because you think Eruv should have everything.

Laura   Not everything. But quite a lot, yes . . . Home and the world. My mum . . . All kinds of people and colours – mixed until ready.

Hala   You're forgetting safety and defiance.

Laura   I'm not. I remember risk and nervousness too.

Anna   That's a lot to hold in a net.

Laura   But it's what I learned from you, taller sister and teacher Hala: how we'll never turn the planet without a mighty imagination. It's here in Eruv, because the net's a teacher too.

Anna   And look! Out there. The others are coming. It's Hanadi on skates and Kate with her harness and shell.

Hala   I hear something else.

Below, the **Immigration Officer** *returns and goes to the foot of Eruv, centre stage. He wears a rope over his shoulder and totes garden shears. With both hands, he carries a high-tech machine, sleek but slightly obsolete, which he sets carefully on the ground. He points its antennae to the upper Eruv. Then he takes out his phone and taps.*

Officer   Yes. In situ and all serene, *sir*. As the Tupper likes to say, no place to run, nowhere to hide. Vigilance. Total eyes and ears and global positioning. I wait; you circle. Only move in emergency. I'm your man, sir. I'm your total man.

Quickly he goes to the net. Notices a water canteen hanging on a hook. Lifts it.

What's *this*? Precious fluid, left for anyone to thieve.

Anna *(from above and behind)*   We take good care. Share a taste before you leave.

He twists the cap from the canteen, gives a shake, then pours the water on the stage.

Officer   Not necessary. We keep our own, down station way. Every drop under lock and key.

Tossing the canteen aside, he moves to the net with shears taken from a back pocket. He cuts a piece on the right, and the left, steps forward into the thicket, and calls up.

Ms Hala, we can finish now. Once you see it's curtains, you don't have to shiver and wriggle. Let yourself go. We'll take care of the rest.

He puts a foot on a cord and reaches to one higher up, shaking the net as he moves. His phone rings. He glances but ignores it.

Because really, it's not your perfect world out there, *is it now?* People don't go strolling across yon border. And pitch their tent in any garden patch. Not if someone's already tilling the soil. With honest sweat of their brow.

Getting balance, he climbs a couple of rungs up, talking as he awkwardly goes.

I found a place of my own, out Putney way. Bit of green, close to the rail, proper homestead, a place to stand. Pater used to say, 'At end of the day, it's squares and rectangles, how you chalk and hold them'. A simple problem, Ms Hala, with a solution you can print on a T-shirt. We want the same thing . . . and one of us happens to have it.

Anna   You seem to like your work.

Officer   I like the duty chart, the office caff, and the khaki. The spiff. The tech. Also why not say it? – I like the chase. It's a riddle, tracking your Hala, but once you find her, it gets very primal very quickly.

Hala   You may be close, but I've learned that getting close is only getting closer, till you get there. And until you do, you're just a thing in an Eruv.

Laura   You said she was innocent. Irises cleared.

Officer   She was. You *were*, Ms Hala. But no more. We moved the goalposts at staff meeting. All change. You're guilty again.

He climbs another rung.

Laura   My mum warned me about men like you, the climbing sharks who cut with their badge.

Officer   If necessary, only if necessary . . . But always a pleasure.

Laura   Mum must have known what Eruv could do. If she were alive, she'd flay you, flank by flank. Just by talking.

Officer   Thirty years for flank-flaying.

Laura   We have nets for the likes of you.

Officer   You're all tongue

Laura   You're flank.

Anna   He reminds me of the phoney pilgrims at monastery. The way the lips crimp.

He thrashes in her direction. He comes across the group of 'cousins' and grabs at several, looking for **Hala**.

Officer   No, not you, I know her scent!

Hala (*from the other side*)   It's salt and the wind . . . You should come to my country. We'll let you in.

He flips in the netting and turns toward her. The cousins (represented through effigies, light effects, the ripple of the net of any other suitable means) obstruct and irritate him with deliberate awkwardness.

Officer   Leave off!

Hala   I've known life after loss.

Officer   You're a nonsense.

Hala (*gazing above the audience*)   I'm alive. And when the sun strikes the knot, you can see the golden world.

Officer *reaches left and right.*

Officer   We have five agents on the ready. But we won't need them, will we, Badri Hala?

Hala   Let me be.

Officer   Never.

Hala   It's not enough to pound your chest? Do you have to eat my heart out too?

Officer   Past time to be getting generous, Madam B.

Steps another rung upwards.

Laura   You need to take care, Mr Officer. We're higher than you think. Shake too hard and Eruv topples, and where would Putney be then?

Anna   It's not too late. It's Eruv here . . . You can serve a higher law.

Officer   Spare me the sermon. (*Halfway up, he turns to face the audience, holding strands with each hand.*) I must have been nine or ten – not more. I was football mad, small for my age, but a cheetah! *Chee*-tah. The teacher ticked my name for room captain, it was the making of me. First choice and final decision: be criminal or the police. I liked spilling soup, but even better was a captain's voice telling some prat to clean the mess. Done in a flash: I saw how rules cut deeper than a knife . . .

Rustling in the net, and the **Officer** *inching higher.*

Hala   We know how it is. No one's born evil; there's time to wind it back.

Anna   Because nothing's decided. The cement's warm, you can change on a penny.

Officer   Not so easy, because why would I want to?

Anna   Because you can. You're a pisser, you kick them up the arse. Look at you – who said you'd stay in place, good porcelain soldier, and now you're too high to climb down. You're rebel, not soldier! *Join us.* Stitch a line of Eruv.

Officer   You're right about one thing.

Anna   Yes?

Officer (*unsteady and giddy in the net*)   I'm starting to feel I've never been anywhere else. This could possibly be it, is what I'm thinking . . .

Pause.

What were we talking about? Who gave me the part of last bastard?

Anna   You took it first audition.

Officer   Did I? Must have. Which is why you lose while I . . . lose less.

He glances down.

Hala   Don't look. It gets steep down there.

Laura   Also long and slow. It's been ages since you took the first step, Officer Oblong. You're older than you know . . .

Officer, *losing control, reaches toward* **Hala** *wildly.*

Hala   You don't need to hurt me. I'm already bleeding.

Anna (*looking down at his distress*)   We've known you forever. Every knot's a thousand years.

Laura   It's past time for you to hatch – and tomorrow wake a gentle bird. You'll be the new chick, fluttering our way. You're free.

Officer   Free? Not bloody likely. Not when you get thirsty like this.

Wipes sweat off his brow with a free hand.

Anna   Think more, it's getting late, and we have nuts and figs galore. Be Eruv.

Officer   Be still!

Beat.

I'm not the hero of our time, only Lieutenant Rules-Keeper.

Laura   But don't you hear them down below. (*Looking at audience.*) They're the ones who know the ropes.

He twists and with difficulty climbs some more. We can see he's reaching a body hidden in the Eruv. Then we see **Laura** *pushing at* *him with both hands. For a full minute, confusion everywhere in the Eruv – everyone moves and thrashes, and finally the* **Officer** *gets close to* **Hala***.*

Hala (*head showing*)   How dare you? How dare you chase a woman through the net?

Anna (*showing her head at the centre*)   We see where you fit.

Laura *shoves at him hard. He doesn't fall, just hangs at a skewed angle, holding on, facing audience, fully extended. A few nuts drop from above.*

Sirens and shaking in the upper strands of the Eruv. Then abrupt silence.

Hala (*unseen and triumphant*)   Over here. Can't you see!

Nuts and figs rain down.

End.